100 Greatest Ideas ... in an instant!

Whether you're a first time manager or an experienced leader, running a small team or an entire organization, straightforward, practical advice is hard to find.

John Adair's 100 Greatest Ideas ... are the building blocks for an amazing career, putting essential business skills and must-have thinking at your fingertips.

The ideas are short, punchy and clustered around themes, so you'll find answers to all your questions quickly and easily. Everything you need to be simply brilliant is here, and it's yours in an instant.

Look out for these at-a-glance features:

Personal Mantra –
Powerful statements as a source for inspiration

Ask Yourself –
Questions to get you thinking about the most information

Remind Yourself –
Key points to help you reflect on the Ideas

Checklist –
A list of questions to help you put the Ideas into practice

100 Greatest Ideas … 6 Great Books

- *John Adair's 100 Greatest Ideas for Effective Leadership*
- *John Adair's 100 Greatest Ideas for Personal Success*
- *John Adair's 100 Greatest Ideas for Brilliant Communication*
- *John Adair's 100 Greatest Ideas for Smart Decision Making*
- *John Adair's 100 Greatest Ideas for Amazing Creativity*
- *John Adair's 100 Greatest Ideas for Being a Brilliant Manager*

JOHN ADAIR'S

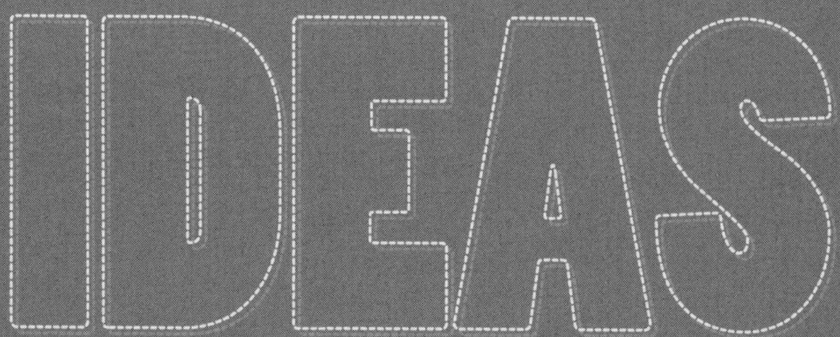

100 GREATEST IDEAS FOR EFFECTIVE LEADERSHIP

CAPSTONE

This edition first published 2011

Registered office
Capstone Publishing Ltd. (A Wiley Company), The Atrium, Southern Gate, Chichester, West Sussex, PO19 8SQ, United Kingdom

For details of our global editorial offices, for customer services and for information about how to apply for permission to reuse the copyright material in this book please see our website at www.wiley.com.

Library of Congress Cataloging-in-Publication Data

Adair, John Eric, 1934– author.
John Adair's 100 Greatest Ideas for Effective Leadership / Mr. John Adair.
p. cm
Includes index.
ISBN 978-0-85708-134-6 (pbk.)
1. Leadership. I. Title. II. Title: John Adair's Hundred Greatest Ideas for Effective Leadership. III. Title: 100 Greatest Ideas for Effective Leadership. IV. Title: Hundred Greatest Ideas for Effective Leadership.
HD57.7J2752 2011
658.4'092–dc22

2010049609

9780857081346 (paperback), 9780857081384 (epub), 9780857081391 (emobi), 9780857081568 (ebook)

A catalogue record for this book is available from the British Library.

Set in 10/13 pt Calibri by Toppan Best-set Premedia Limited

Printed in the United Kingdom by TJ International, Padstow, Cornwall.

Author's Note

Effective business people have fine-tuned leadership and management ability backed up by exceptional decision-making, communication and creative skills and the know-how to implement it all successfully. These six areas are the basis of the 100 Greatest series.

None of these skills stands alone, each is interconnected, and for that reason I've revisited key ideas across the series. If you read more than one book, as I hope you will, you'll meet key ideas more than once. These are the framework on which the series hang and the repetition will help you become a master of modern business.

Likewise, if you only read one book, the inclusion of key ideas from across the series means that you'll benefit from seeing your chosen subject within the wider context of Leadership and Management excellence.

Good luck on your journey to becoming an effective manager within your organization.

John Adair

Contents

Preface

> *Listen to all, pluck a feather from every passing goose, but follow no one absolutely.*
>
> Chinese proverb

It is with great pleasure that I offer you my *100 Greatest Ideas on Effective Leadership*. Please pluck as many feathers as you like from this collection and make them your own. I hope that they will enrich your personal effectiveness as a leader.

The basic units of the book are the Ideas, which are grouped together under themes and also divided into Parts. As you will see, the Ideas vary considerably. Some consist of just one simple idea. Others are more like 'cluster bombs': smaller ideas about an important element. Whatever their size or shape, they all have relevance to your journey of leadership.

This book takes a logical look at those issues that you have to get to grips with to perform well as a leader.

To be successful as a leader, you have to be well organized and disciplined; good at goal setting and focused on objectives; able to think creatively and make decisions; and able to communicate with other people.

The Ideas presented here are a distillation of my greatest tried-and-tested ideas in all these areas and will help you to function better as

a leader or manager. You'll be better able to get results through people and also to understand yourself and others.

The book does not debate at length the differences between being a manager and being a leader – the approach is rather the practical one that these greatest ideas will serve to improve your personal performance as both a manager and a leader.

In these pages I hope you will find inspiration to persevere until you achieve excellence as an effective leader.

John Adair

PART ONE

Understanding Leadership

My greatest discovery by far has been regarding what people now call the generic role of *leader*, the role that is common to all working groups and organizations anywhere in the world.

At the heart of that role lie the three overlapping core responsibilities of any leader: achieving the task, building and maintaining the team, and developing the individual.

This model implies an understanding of the environment in which you are working. In order to fulfil these responsibilities, you need to know your business, and you need to possess or develop the necessary qualities of personality, character and skills to provide the eight generic leadership functions: defining the task, planning, briefing, controlling, evaluating, supporting, motivating, and setting an example.

The three circles of leadership functions integrate together what we customarily call leadership and management, but these concepts do retain their own distinct overtones:

- *Leading* is about giving direction, especially in times of change; inspiring or motivating people to work willingly; building and maintaining teamwork; and providing an example, producing a personal output – or doing some of the work yourself.
- *Managing* is about running the business in 'steady-state' conditions; day-to-day administration; organizing structures and establishing systems; and controlling, especially by financial methods.

Both sets of skills and activities are essential. You have to be a manager-leader or a leader-manager, depending on your specific role and/or your level of responsibility in the organization.

'Management is prose, leadership is poetry.'

Five Greatest Ideas for Understanding the Functions of Leadership

Idea 1: Task, team and individual

In leadership there are always three interacting elements or variables:

1 The leader: qualities of personality and character.
2 The situation: partly constant, partly varying.
3 The group: the followers, their needs and values.

It is helpful to look at leadership in relation to the needs of work groups. Work groups are always unique – they have their own group personality – but like individuals, they share needs in common:

1 Task need: to achieve the common task.
2 Team maintenance needs: to be held together or to be maintained as a team.
3 Individual needs: the needs that individuals bring with them into the group.

These three needs (the task, the team and the individual) are now the watchwords of leadership and people expect their leaders to:

- Help them achieve the common task.
- Build the synergy of teamwork.
- Respond to individuals and meet their needs.

Why *needs*? Working groups come into being because there is a task to be done that one person cannot do on their own. A pressure to accomplish it builds up. If the group is prevented from completing the task, it will experience frustration.

The other two needs are more below the surface. Groups are prone to fragmentation, and the forces that are holding them together –

team maintenance – need to be stronger than the forces that are pushing them apart. The creation, promotion and retention of group/ organizational cohesiveness are essential, on the principle of 'united we stand, divided we fall'.

The *individual* needs are the physical ones (e.g. salary) and the more psychological ones of:

- Recognition.
- A sense of doing something worthwhile.
- Status.
- The deeper need to give and to receive from other people in a working situation.

Task, team and individual needs overlap, as in the diagram.

For example:

- Achieving the task builds the team and satisfies the individuals.

- If team maintenance fails (the team lacks cohesiveness), performance on the task is impaired and individual satisfaction is reduced.
- If individual needs are not met, the team will lack cohesiveness and performance of the task will be impaired.

When approaching business problems, issues or situations, do I always think: task, team and individual?

Idea 2: Leadership function – action-centred leadership

At whatever level of leadership you are, you must continually think about task, team and individual needs. To achieve the common task, maintain teamwork and satisfy individuals, certain functions have to be performed. A *function* is what leaders *do* as opposed to a *quality*, which is an aspect of what they *are*.

These functions (the *functional approach* to leadership, also called *action-centred leadership*) are:

- *Defining the task:* What are the purpose, aims and objectives? Why is this work worthwhile?
- *Planning:* A plan answers the question of *how* you are going to get from where you are now to where you want to be. There is nothing like a bad plan to break up a group or frustrate individuals.
- *Briefing:* The ability to communicate, to get across to people the task and the plan.
- *Controlling:* Making sure that all resources and energies are properly harnessed.
- *Supporting:* Setting and maintaining organizational and team values and standards.
- *Motivating:* Gaining the goodwill and wholehearted commitment of the team and each individual member.
- *Evaluating:* Establishing and applying the success criteria appropriate to the field.
- *Setting an example:* Leading from the front while exemplifying the qualities and behaviours expected in the team.

Leadership functions in relation to task, team and individual can be represented by the following diagram.

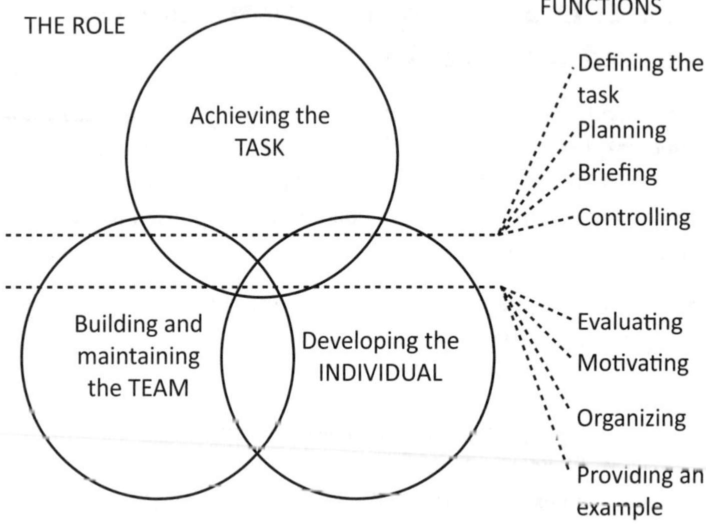

These leadership functions need to be completed with excellence. You achieve this by performing the functions with increasing skill and also by regularly reviewing and reflecting on your performance.

Before examining the skills of leadership, it is worth seeing which qualities of personality or character can be viewed as having functional value. These are traditionally called the qualities or characteristics of leadership. Again, they can be split into task, team and individual elements.

Idea 3: Leadership characteristics – task element

Before you can start to develop skills in leadership, you need to identify certain key qualities and typical outcomes that these qualities achieve when managing tasks.

The need	Quality	Functional value
Task	Initiative	Getting the group moving
	Perseverance	Preventing the group giving up
	Efficiency	Getting work done well, knowing costs (energy, time, money)
	Honesty	Establishing facts
	Self-confidence	Facing facts
	Industry	Reaping dividends through steady application
	Audacity	Not being restrained by rules or convention
	Humility	Facing up to mistakes and not blaming others

How many of these qualities do I possess? How can I develop those I don't and improve those I do?

Idea 4: Leadership characteristics – team element

These are the key qualities needed to build and run a team successfully:

The need	Quality	Functional value
Team	Integrity	Integrating the team and creating trust
	Humour	Relieving tension and maintaining a sense of proportion
	Audacity	Inspiring through originality or verve
	Self-confidence	Fostering trust in others
	Justice	Building group discipline through fair dealing
	Honesty	Winning respect
	Humility	Not being selfish, arrogant or divisive, and sharing praise

When was the last time I laughed with a colleague in the office? Do I take myself too seriously?

'United we stand, divided we fall.'

Idea 5: Leadership characteristics – individual element

Dealing successfully with individuals is very different from dealing with your team as a group, although justice is common to both. Somehow you've got to balance the qualities of self-confidence and audacity with those of compassion and humility if you're to do the job really well.

The need	Quality	Functional value
Individual	Tact	Being sensitive in dealing with people
	Compassion	Showing sympathetic awareness and help
	Consistency	Enabling people to know where they stand
	Humility	Recognizing qualities/abilities and giving credit
	Honesty	Winning individual respect
	Justice	Encouraging individuals through fair dealing

Whilst the whole may be greater than the sum of the parts, the whole is made up of parts – each individual contribution counts.

Follow-up test

The three circles model

- ☐ Have you been able to give specific examples from your own experience on how the three circles or areas of need – task, team and individual – interact with each other?
- ☐ Can you identify your natural bias:
  - ◆ You tend to put the task first, and are low on team and individual.
  - ◆ For you the team seems more important: you value happy relationships more than productivity or individual job satisfaction.
  - ◆ Individuals are supremely important to you: you always put the individual before the task or the team, for that matter. You tend to over-identify with the individual.
  - ◆ You can honestly say that you maintain a balance, and have feedback from superiors, colleagues and subordinates to prove it.

Leadership functions

1 What function of the eight do you perform at present with the most skill?

2 Have others commented favourably on your actions as a leader in that respect?

3 What function do you most tend to neglect?

Leadership qualities

Of the sixteen different characteristics listed in Ideas 3, 4 and 5, identify your personal top five and your bottom five.

Top five:

1
2
3
4
5

Bottom five:

1
2
3
4
5

Check your list with a friend who knows you well.

'Leadership is action, not position.'

PART TWO

Performing as a Leader

The greatest ideas for performing as a leader are grouped under the key areas of setting and achieving objectives, developing leadership skills and the essential qualities of leadership.

Once you have a clear idea of the generic role and responsibilities of a leader, you need to build up your knowledge of your own strengths and weaknesses (or areas for improvement) *in relation to that role*.

When you identify your personal goals there should always be, I suggest, at least one that relates to learning and self-development. In the speech that President John F Kennedy was on his way to deliver in Dallas when he was shot dead on that fateful day, he was going to say: 'Leadership and learning are indispensable to each other.' Let his words live today.

Focus your attention on developing your skills for the key functions that are part of the generic leadership role. That is the best

foundation for leadership effectiveness. Once you can perform these functions with real skill when required, you can then progress rapidly to excellence. You can, for example, transcend the basics of motivating people and begin to inspire them – and be inspired by them.

It may seem virtually impossible to develop leadership qualities by any kind of deliberate effort – and it is certainly something that happens over a long period of time. All I can do here is draw your attention to their importance.

Reflective thinking on your part is the best way to open the door and – over time – to invite these qualities into your house.

> *Personally I am always ready to learn, although I do not always like being taught.*
>
> Sir Winston Churchill

Three Greatest Ideas for Setting and Achieving Your Objectives

Idea 6: Draw up a personal profile

The starting point is to do a self-assessment and take stock of yourself in the overall context of the direction you would like to be heading. Bear in mind the generic role of a leader described in Part One. What natural strengths and weaknesses do you bring to that role?

Personal Role

1. What are my strengths/what special skills do I have?
2. What are my values (i.e. what is important and worthwhile to me)?
3. What would be my preferred ways of earning a living?
4. What activities/situations do I want to avoid?
5. What achievements would I like to list as having been successfully met in my life?
6. What would I like the highlights of my obituary to be? (This is a really good way of focusing the mind, as is asking yourself how you would like your epitaph to read.)

Do I regularly take stock of my skills, values and preferences?

Idea 7: Set personal goals

Answering the questions in Idea 6 will enable you to set out more clearly the goals and objectives you want to achieve in your life and, linked with your time management skills, plan the important steps you need to take to achieve them. You will then be able to 'add years to your life and more life to your years'.

The approach is to work from the long term back to the short term, as follows:

1 What are my lifetime goals/objectives?
2 What are my five-year goals/objectives?
3 What goals/objectives will I set for achievement within one year?

Taking this approach will ensure that you concentrate on those goals/objectives that are important to you. The strategic element of your approach will then ensure that you analyze the obstacles that you have to overcome and plan your priorities and the ways/means to achieve your one-year, five-year and lifetime goals/objectives.

For each set of goals/objectives:

1 Have I identified obstacles and opportunities?
2 What are the ways/means to achieve goals/objectives, despite/because of those obstacles/opportunities?

This will give you your plan(s) for how to achieve your personal goals and objectives – which you must then implement!

Set goals and measure your progress toward them – and be prepared to review the goals themselves for their continuing relevance.

Idea 8: Set professional business goals

As you have seen, your strategic aims result from asking these questions:

- Where are we now?
- Where do we want to be in three or five years' time?
- What strengths and weaknesses do we have?
- How can we improve?
- Can we get to where we want to be?

Similar to setting personal goals/objectives, delineate your professional business goals/objectives (for your organization and, perhaps separately, for yourself at work):

1 What are the key long-term goals/objectives?
2 What are the five-year goals/objectives?
3 What are the one-year goals/objectives?

Then plans and strategies have to be addressed, as in:

1 Identifying obstacles and opportunities.
2 Analyzing ways/means to achieve goals/objectives despite/because of those obstacles/opportunities.

Planning answers the question: *How are we going to achieve* a particular task, meet a goal or reach an objective? How leads to who, what and when? You can then set out your strategy for achieving:

- Short-term goals/objectives – for one year.
- Medium-term goals/objectives – for five years.
- Long-term goals/objectives.

Goals/objectives must be clear, specific, measurable, attainable, written, time-bounded, realistic, challenging, agreed, consistent, worthwhile and participative.

Attaining goals/objectives brings into play strategy and planning, for which you need imagination, a sense of reality, the power of analysis and what has been described as helicopter vision (the ability to see matters in detail, but from a higher perspective).

Of course, you can't spend all your time planning – you need to attain the right balance between planning and implementation. Planning saves time at the strategic and operational level and the key principle is that every moment spent planning saves three or four moments in execution.

'The world makes way for the person who knows where they are going.'

Nine Greatest Ideas for Leadership Skills

This section covers the eight functions of leadership: defining the task, planning, briefing, controlling, evaluating, supporting, motivating, and setting an example. It ends with the Adair short course on leadership, which is especially useful in carrying out the briefing function.

Am I a born leader yet?

Idea 9: Defining the task

Keep the general goals in sight while tackling daily tasks.

Chinese proverb

A task is something that needs to be done. People in organizations and teams need to have this distilled into an objective, which is:

- Clear.
- Concrete.
- Time-limited.
- Realistic.
- Challenging.
- Capable of evaluation

This is not *my* task, it is *our* task – we share it because it has a value for the organization and ourselves.

There are five tests to apply when defining a task:

1. Do you have a clear idea of the objectives of your group now and for the next few years/months, and have these been agreed with your boss?
2. Do you understand the overall aims and purpose of the organization?
3. Can you set your group's objectives into the context of those larger intentions?
4. Is your present main objective specific, defined in terms of time and as concrete/tangible as you can make it?

5 Will the team know for itself if it succeeds or fails and does it get speedy feedback on results?

In defining the task/communicating the objective, you need to have the following abilities:

- Telling the group the objectives you have been given.
  Beware: Not understanding an objective yourself can lead to lack of clarity.
- Telling the group what to do and why.
  Beware: Giving the reason in terms of a past event rather than the future.
- Breaking down aims into objectives for other groups.
  Beware: Not making them specific enough or not making sure there are enough objectives that add up to complete the aim.
- Agreeing the objective.
  Beware: Taking things for granted and not fixing on the objective.
- Relating the aim to the purpose (to answer what and why questions).
  Beware: Confusing your division's aim with the purpose of the organization.
- Defining the purpose and checking that the aims relate to it and to each other.
  Beware: Not doing it often enough.
- Redefining the purpose to generalize it and creating more aims and objectives.
  Beware: Causing confusion by doing it too often, or not knowing that it has to be done.
- Communicating purpose to employees.
  Beware: Using the wrong language, by-passing leaders below you, or relying on others to do it for you.

One vital question that a leader should be able to answer up-front is: 'How will we know when we have succeeded?' In other words, *what are the success criteria?* If that question cannot be answered, it is usually a sign that the task is not yet clear enough.

Defining the task is not something you have to do only at the beginning of an enterprise – confusion about the end of a task can soon invade a group or organization. So you should be ready to define the end that the team or any given individual is presently working toward whenever the need arises.

Idea 10: Planning

I keep six honest serving men
(They taught me all I knew);
Their names are What *and* Why *and* When,
And How *and* Where *and* Who.

Rudyard Kipling

Planning is the activity of bridging the tap mentally from where you and the group are now to where you want to be at some future moment in terms of accomplishing a task.

'Fail to plan and you plan to fail.'

A poor or inadequate plan means that your subsequent team action is doomed from the start. It usually turns into a drama – a comedy or a tragedy, depending on the circumstances – in three Acts: Beginning, Muddle and No End.

This key activity of planning for any team or organization requires a search for alternatives and that is best done with others in an open-minded, encouraging and creative way. Foreseeable contingencies should always be planned for.

Checklist for planning

- ☐ Have I called on specialist advice?
- ☐ Have all feasible courses of action been considered and weighed up in terms of resources needed/available and outcomes?
- ☐ Has a programme been established that will achieve the objective?
- ☐ Is there a provision for contingencies?
- ☐ Were more creative solutions searched for as a basis for the plan?
- ☐ Is the plan simple and as foolproof as possible, rather than complicated?
- ☐ Does the plan include necessary preparation or training for the team and its members?

In ensuring that there is the appropriate level of participation in the planning process, the planning continuum chart may be useful.

The planning continuum

Any decision can be shared in the way set out in the planning continuum. The more that as a leader you share a decision, the greater the motivation of the team but the less control you have on the quality of the resulting decision. Your aim should be dependent on the time available and the knowledge/experience of the team – both high commitment and high quality.

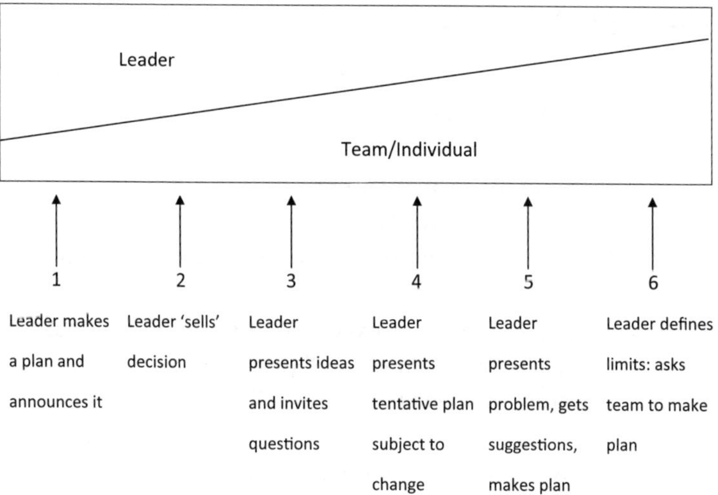

Take a leaf out of Napoleon's book – think ahead and visualize what may arise as you implement the plan:

> *If I always appear prepared, it is because, before entering on an undertaking, I have meditated for long and have foreseen what may occur. It is not genius which reveals to me suddenly and secretly what I should do in circumstances unexpected by others; it is thought and meditation.*

Idea 11: Briefing

Briefing or instructing a team is a basic leadership function, usually conducted face to face. A briefing is an opportunity to:

- Create the right atmosphere.
- Promote teamwork.
- Get to know, encourage and motivate each individual.

Before and after any briefing session, in order to ensure that the question of 'what is my role in all this?' (which will be on everyone's mind) is answered, you need to ask yourself these questions:

1 Does every individual know exactly what his/her job is?
2 Does each member of the team have clearly defined targets and performance standards agreed with me?
3 Does each person clearly know at the end what is expected of him/her and how that contribution or that of his/her team fits in with the purposeful work of everyone else?

Communicating (speaking and listening) is crucial to get right in any briefing and it centres on the task, team and individual needs that should be addressed.

The effective speaking attributes of a successful briefing are to be:

- Prepared.
- Clear.
- Simple.
- Vivid.
- Natural.
- Concise.

Can you think of one example from your own experience of briefings that fitted this description – and maybe one that fell far short of it?

Showing confidence is always important, for example when explaining the task and the role of the team/individual, and especially in an initial briefing or where there is low morale.

You don't have to be a great orator, but do put your message across in a clear, compelling and positive way. In ancient Athens, Demosthenes once said to a rival orator:

> *You make the audience say, 'How well he speaks!' I make them say, 'Let us march against Philip [king of Macedonia]!'*

Can I speak in a way that moves the team to take the desired action?

At all levels of leadership responsibility there are individuals who need to be briefed in clear and simple language. Such occasions – team, organizational or individual – are not to be seen merely in terms of the task. They are also opportunities for you to create the right *atmosphere*, to promote *teamwork*, and to get to know, encourage and motivate each *individual* person. There will be more suggestions on all of these areas later in the book.

Idea 12: Controlling

To know how to do it is simple – the difficulty is doing it.

Chinese proverb

Once work has started on a project it is vital that you *control* and *coordinate* what is being done, so that everyone's energy is turning wheels and making things happen. The synergy or common energy of the group should be fully deployed in implementing the common plan and producing the desired results.

How do you do that? The secret of controlling is to have a clear idea in your mind of what should be happening, when it should occur, who should be doing it, and how it should be done.

The more effectively you have involved the group in your planning, the more likely it is that they too will have a similar picture of what is required.

Excellent leaders get maximum results with the minimum of resources.

To control others, leaders need to exhibit self-control. Nevertheless, remembering that anger and sadness can be legitimate responses if the circumstances warrant it, and that they are themselves mechanisms for control.

Leaders also need to have good control systems (simple and effective in monitoring both financial and task performance) and to have control of what others should and should not be doing in order to meet objectives. The degree of success in directing, regulating, restraining or encouraging individuals and coordinating or harmonizing team efforts on the task (and in meetings) is the criterion for testing a leader's effectiveness as a 'controller'.

Can I rely on the team as a whole and its individual members to carry through what they have committed themselves to do 'until it be thoroughly finished'?

The idea is that the team or the individual with whom you are dealing should become *self-controlling*, so they can regulate their own performance against standards or the clock. They'll say things like: 'We have only got two hours left, so we will have to work harder to get the job done to meet the deadline.' Your aim as a leader is to intervene as little as possible.

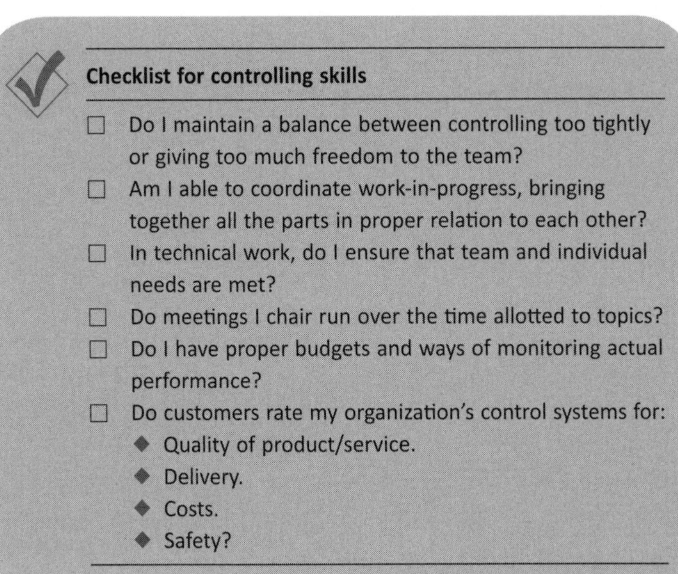

Checklist for controlling skills

- ☐ Do I maintain a balance between controlling too tightly or giving too much freedom to the team?
- ☐ Am I able to coordinate work-in-progress, bringing together all the parts in proper relation to each other?
- ☐ In technical work, do I ensure that team and individual needs are met?
- ☐ Do meetings I chair run over the time allotted to topics?
- ☐ Do I have proper budgets and ways of monitoring actual performance?
- ☐ Do customers rate my organization's control systems for:
  - Quality of product/service.
  - Delivery.
  - Costs.
  - Safety?

Steer between the two rocks of too much interference and lack of direction.

Idea 13: Evaluating

Leaders need to be good at:

- Assessing *consequences*.
- Evaluating team *performance*.
- Appraising and training *individuals*.
- Judging *people*.

In assessing consequences, leaders should be able to foresee the outcome of action (or inaction) in terms of the technical, the financial and the human aspects of a particular activity, and to ask probing questions of the team in order to establish the likely consequences.

In evaluating team performance, perhaps through a debriefing session after a particular project, the performance of the team as a whole in relation to the task can be examined:

- Has it been a success, a partial success or a failure?
- Can lessons be learnt?
- Can action be taken to improve performance?
- What feedback can be given to ensure improvement?

Evaluating the team is helpful in trying to build it into a high-performance one, the hallmarks of which are:

- Clear, realistic objectives.
- A shared sense of purpose.
- The best use of resources.
- An atmosphere of openness.
- The capacity to handle failure.
- The ability to ride out storms.

In appraising and training individuals, the following framework can be used:

- Assessment of past performance.
- Outline of future work to be done: targets, priorities, standards and strategies.
- Matching perceptions of what can be expected by each party of the other in order to achieve a good working relationship.
- Improving skill, knowledge, and behaviour.

Some tips for handling appraisals:

- Have all the necessary data available.
- Put the other person at ease.
- Control the pace and direction of the interview.
- Listen, listen, listen.
- Avoid destructive criticism, but encourage self-criticism.
- Review performance systematically.
- Discuss future action.
- Discuss the individual's potential and aspirations.
- Identify training or development required.
- Avoid common pitfalls, such as:
  - Dominating the conversation.
  - Making promises that are unlikely to be kept.
  - Expecting dramatic changes overnight.
  - Blaming those who are not present.

In judging people, leaders decide who should do what. This always affects outcomes and so is a crucial skill.

Leaders should not have favourites because:

- It destroys team unity.
- The favourite is a personification of your judgement about people – if others do not agree with your judgement, your credibility suffers.
- Favourites advance by recognizing the social and esteem needs of their bosses and pandering to them – the boss can have his/her judgement impaired by this.

You can improve your judgement by analyzing the impressions you have formed and discussing them with others, and by making decisions about people more slowly and after deliberation.

In evaluation, you need to ensure that:

- Your decision making shows good judgement.
- You appraise people regularly and well.
- You are good at judging people.
- You evaluate your own performance as much as those who work for you.

Do I also apply the principle of evaluation to myself and my work?

Idea 14: Supporting

Ducere est servire (To lead is to serve)

Motto of Britain's Chartered Institute of Management

Supporting is a broad function, covering many of the actions that you will take in team and individual circles. Setting and maintaining group standards – the invisible rules that bind a group together – by word and example, for instance, is a form of supporting, as is giving help to an individual in time of need.

There is a Japanese proverb that says: 'If he works for you, you work for him.' Leadership is done from in front... yes, but sometimes you have to stand behind your people and always to be ready to stand by them.

One critical way in which a leader supports the team or organization is to shoulder the whole weight of failure.

After General Wolfe's first attack on Quebec had failed, he wrote:

> *The blame I take entirely upon my shoulders, and I expect to suffer for it. Accidents cannot be helped. As much of the plan as was defective falls justly on me.*

Sometimes people can be weighed down by the difficulty of the task. Here supporting takes the form of *encouraging* the whole team or perhaps a struggling individual. Words are not always necessary; sometimes the very presence of a good leader relieves the pressure.

In his novel *Typhoon*, Joseph Conrad graphically describes the relief provided by a first mate in a severe gale:

> *Jukes was uncritically glad to have his captain at hand. It relieved him as though that man had, by simply coming on deck, taken at once most of the gale's weight upon his shoulders. Such is the prestige, the privilege, and the burden of command.*

Checklist for supporting skills

- ☐ Have I created a supportive, warm climate in the organization, so that each member willingly helps their neighbour?
- ☐ Do the written and unwritten codes of behaviour support the best for task, team and individual?
- ☐ Am I supportive of individuals who are going through a difficult time in their personal lives?
- ☐ Do I fully accept the 'burden of command' when things go wrong?
- ☐ Does my presence calm things down in a crisis – or make it worse?

Idea 15: Motivating

There are six key principles for motivating others:

1. Be motivated yourself.
2. Select people who are highly motivated.
3. Set realistic and challenging targets.
4. Remember that progress motivates.
5. Provide fair rewards.
6. Give recognition.

Individuals are motivated by their requirement to satisfy a hierarchy of needs, such as that described by Maslow (more on this in Idea 30):

- Physiological – hunger, thirst, sleep.
- Safety – security, protection from danger.
- Social – belonging, acceptance, social life, friendship and love.
- Esteem – self-respect, achievement, status, recognition.
- Self-actualization – growth, accomplishment, personal development.

Each individual will be at a different stage or level on this hierarchy of needs and will have their own inner pattern of motivational needs.

Other than in financial terms, individuals are usually motivated if they can see that they will be given:

- Achievement.
- Recognition.
- Job interest.
- Responsibility.
- Advancement.

A good leader provides both the right context and climate and at least some of the opportunities for these individual needs to be met. This is perhaps the most difficult but also the most rewarding of a leader's challenges.

> *'You do not need a whip to urge on an obedient horse.'*
>
> Russian proverb

Idea 16: Setting an example

The lantern carrier should go ahead.

Japanese proverb

'Leadership is example.' To be successful a good leader must 'walk the talk'. Employees take a fraction of the time to get to know a leader that the leader takes to get to know them. The example you are giving is quite simply *you*. Whether this is a good or a bad example depends on you, the leader.

An example is set in verbal and non-verbal ways and all aspects of a leader's words and deeds must be considered in the light of this fact.

And if an example is contagious, it is worth ensuring that you set a good one to encourage the qualities that you seek in others.

Some key questions for good leadership are:

- Task – do you lead from the front/by example?
- Team – do you develop your team's standards through the power of example?
- Individual – do you view each individual as a leader in their own right?

Bad examples, particularly of hypocrisy, are noticed more than good ones, so leaders must take care in all they say and do.

I cannot hear what you are saying to me because what you are is shouting at me.

Zulu proverb

- Do I set a good example?
- Do I ask others to do what I would be unwilling to do myself?
- Do people comment on the good example I set in my work?
- Does my (bad) example conflict with what everyone is trying to do?
- Can I quote when I last deliberately set out to give a leading example?
- Do I mention the importance of example to team leaders who report to me?

Idea 17: The Adair short course on leadership

The six most important words: 'I admit I made a mistake.'
The five most important words: 'I am proud of you.'
The four most important words: 'What is your opinion?'
The three most important words: 'If you please.'
The two most important words: 'Thank you.'
The one most important word: 'We.'
And the one least important word: 'I.'

Four Greatest Ideas for Leadership Qualities

Idea 18: The 25 attributes of leadership and management

A survey of successful chief executives about the attributes most valuable at top levels of management indicated the following *in order of rating*:

1. Ability to take decisions.
2. Leadership.
3. Integrity.
4. Enthusiasm.
5. Imagination.
6. Willingness to work hard.
7. Analytical ability.
8. Understanding of others.
9. Ability to spot opportunities.
10. Ability to meet unpleasant situations.
11. Ability to adapt quickly to change.
12. Willingness to take risks.
13. Enterprise.
14. Capacity to speak lucidly.
15. Astuteness.
16. Ability to administer efficiently.
17. Open-mindedness.
18. Ability to 'stick to it'.
19. Willingness to work long hours.
20. Ambition.
21. Single-mindedness.
22. Capacity for lucid writing.
23. Curiosity.
24. Skill with numbers.
25. Capacity for abstract thought.

Am I good at giving direction, providing inspiration, building teams and setting an example?

No list of leadership qualities, however long, is ever complete, though. You should regard this one as an indicative list. Nor should the rating order be taken too seriously. Yet it is the best long list I know of the attributes that you need if you are going to be a great chief executive – and it holds true throughout the world.

Idea 19: The seven qualities of leadership

A leader not only has knowledge and skills, he or she also has the right qualities to lead a group to achieve its ends *willingly*.

Personality and character cannot be left out of leadership. There are certain generic leadership traits. Seven of the most important ones are:

1. *Enthusiasm* – try naming a leader without it!
2. *Integrity* – meaning both personal wholeness and sticking to values outside yourself, primarily goodness and truth. Integrity makes people trust a leader.
3. *Toughness* – being demanding, with high standards, resilient, tenacious and with the aim of being respected (not necessarily popular).
4. *Fairness* – impartial, rewarding/penalizing performance without 'favourites', treating individuals differently but equally. Firm but fair.
5. *Warmth* – the heart as well as the mind being engaged, loving what is being done and caring for people. 'Cold fish' do not make good leaders.
6. *Humility* – the opposite of arrogance, being a listener and without an overpowering ego.
7. *Confidence* – not over-confident (which leads to arrogance), but with a calm self-confidence. People know whether you have confidence or not.

Idea 20: Leadership qualities test

To test whether or not you have the basic qualities of leadership, ask yourself these questions:

- Do I possess the seven qualities outlined in Idea 19?
- Have I demonstrated that I am a responsible person?
- Do I like the responsibility and the rewards of leadership?
- Am I well known for my enthusiasm at work?
- Have I ever been described as having integrity?
- Do I have the toughness and firmness of a good leader? Can I expect and demand the best from people – beginning with myself?
- Am I firm but fair in my dealings with both the team as a whole and each individual member?
- Can I show that people think of me as a warm and kind person?
- Am I an active and socially participative person?
- Do I have the self-confidence to take criticism, indifference and/or unpopularity from others?
- Can I control my emotions and moods or do I let them control me?
- Have I been dishonest or less than straight with people who work for me over the past six months?
- Am I very introvert or very extrovert (or am I an ambivert – a mixture of both – as leaders should be)?

Leadership depends on the situation, so you need to ask yourself, whatever your qualities, whether you are right for the situation you are in:

- Are my interests, aptitudes and temperament suited to my current field of work?

- If not, can I identify one that would better suit me and where I would emerge as a leader?
- Do I have the 'authority of knowledge' in my current field and have I acquired all the necessary professional and specialist skills through training that I could have done at this point in my career?
- Am I experienced in more than one field/industry/function?
- Am I interested in fields adjacent and relevant to my own?
- Do I read situations well and am I flexible in my approach to changes within my field?

Idea 21: Humility in action

A leader is best
When people barely know that he exists,
Not so good when people obey and acclaim him,
Worst when they despise him.
'Fail to honour people,
They fail to honour you';
But of a good leader, who talks little,
When his work is done, his aim fulfilled,
They will all say, 'We did this ourselves.'

Lao Tzu, sixth century BCE

Follow-up test

Personal goals

1 Do you have a definition on paper of your principal purpose or chief aim for your working life?

2 Can you break that down into two or three open-ended aims?

3 Is your assessment of your strengths and weaknesses both positive and realistic?

Organizational goals

- ☐ Are you clear about the objectives of your team now and for the next few years/months, and have you agreed them with your leader?
- ☐ Do you fully understand the wider aims and purpose of the organization?
- ☐ Can you relate the objectives of your team to those larger, more general intentions?

- ☐ Does your present team objective have sufficient specificity? Is it defined in terms of time? Is it as concrete or tangible as you can make it?
- ☐ Will the team be able to know soon for itself if you succeed or fail? Does it have swift feedback of results?

Leadership qualities

1 Do you share the view that in leadership what you are is as important as what you know and what you do?

2 Which three people known to you have you admired most as leaders?

i
ii
iii

3 Can you think of five qualities that they shared in common?

i
ii
iii
iv
v

4 Did any one of them have a positive quality mentioned in Part Two that the other two lacked?

PART THREE

Power Through the People

Worthwhile results as a leader can only be achieved with and through other people. This section looks at how to get the best from other people, particularly examining how best to create great teams and motivate each individual person in the team – including yourself!

Focusing solely on the task and ignoring the team and the individual is a beginner's error in leadership. Alas, there are too many beginners today! Doing this is surprisingly still common – especially when the pressure is on and the stress levels are running high.

In order to motivate people you need to understand how human nature works – and then work with the grain. And you should love people, in the sense that you really want to help them to give their best – for both their and the common good.

We transcend ourselves and we achieve so much more when we are working in a great team. The end-product of excellent leadership is high performance. In Part Three you will find a framework for what such a team looks like, together with some practical steps for developing your team-building skills.

> *If people are of one heart, even the yellow earth can become gold.*
>
> Chinese proverb

Six Greatest Ideas for Teambuilding

Idea 22: Teambuilding – the functions of the leader

'Teamwork is no accident, it is a by-product of good leadership.'

Teambuilding is part of the core organic leadership role: the trinity of task, team and individual.

One of the main results of good leadership is a good team. We talk about what makes a great team in Idea 27, but it can be briefly expressed as:

- having a clear sense of direction and works hard and effectively.
- being confident in its ability to achieve specific, challenging objectives.
- believing in and identifying with the organization.
- holding together when the going gets rough.
- having respect for and trust in its leader.
- adapting to the changing world.

Good leadership characteristics	Team outcomes
Enthusing	Team members are purposefully busy and have a basis for judging priorities
Lives values such as integrity	A sense of excitement and achievement, with people willing to take risks and accept higher workloads

Good leadership characteristics	Team outcomes
Leads by example	Consistency in knowing leader's values
Generates good leaders from followers	A high level of mutual trust
Aware of own behaviour and environment	All members live up to leader's example
Intellect and experience to meet the situational demands	Confidence in leadership
Aware of team and individual needs	The led start to lead with the leader being less prominent, more of a coach and supporter
Exhibits trust	Inspires a climate of confidence and high performance
Represents the organization to the team and vice versa	Confident about contribution to organizational purpose and aims and a high level of commitment to them

In achieving the task, building the team and developing the individual, while you may have your own style as leader, you do have to:

- Be active in setting direction and accepting the risks of leadership.
- Be able to communicate direction and objectives clearly and keep your people in the picture.
- Use the appropriate behaviour to gain commitment for the achievement of specific objectives.
- Maintain high standards of personal performance and demand high standards of performance from others.

Leaders in teambuilding are responsible for ensuring that the key functions are being done properly:

- Defining the task.
- Planning.
- Briefing.
- Controlling.
- Evaluating.
- Supporting.
- Motivating.
- Setting an example.

If you give people respect, trust and some real responsibility, together with a degree of independence, they will reward you by giving their best to the common task and to the team.

The gold-standard leader in teambuilding must act as:

- Encourager.
- Harmonizer.
- Compromiser.
- Bridge builder.
- Expediter/gatekeeper.
- Standard setter.
- Group observer/commentator.
- Catalyst for change.

When leaders are worthy of respect, the people are willing to work for them. When their virtue is worthy of admiration, their authority can be established.

Haunanzi (Chinese philosopher, 4th century BCE)

Idea 23: Achieving the task – with a team

To assess how well you achieve tasks with your team, think about the following questions and answer 'yes' or 'no' to each. For each question that you have answered with a 'no' (or in the case of 'training' and 'supervision' with an unsatisfactory outcome), define how you are going to put things right – and by when.

- ☐ *Purpose*: Am I clear what the task is?
- ☐ *Responsibilities*: Am I clear what mine are?
- ☐ *Objectives*: Have I agreed these with my superior, the person accountable for the group?
- ☐ *Programme*: Have I worked one out to reach objectives?
- ☐ *Working conditions*: Are these right for the job?
- ☐ *Resources*: Are these adequate (authority, money, materials)?
- ☐ *Targets*: Has each member clearly defined and agreed them?
- ☐ *Authority*: Is the line of authority clear (on the accountability chart)?
- ☐ *Training*: Are there any gaps in the specialist skills or abilities of individuals in the group required for the task?
- ☐ *Priorities*: Have I planned the time effectively?
- ☐ *Progress*: Do I check this regularly and evaluate?
- ☐ *Supervision*: In case of my absence, who covers for me?
- ☐ *Example*: Do I set standards by my behaviour?

Idea 24: Building the team

Answer the questions below honestly, 'yes' or 'no'. If the answer is 'no' to any question, work out what you need to do to put matters right – and set yourself an achievable time target within which to do it.

- ☐ *Objectives*: Does the team clearly understand and accept them?
- ☐ *Standards*: Do they know what standards of performance are expected?
- ☐ *Safety standards*: Do they know the consequences of infringement?
- ☐ *Size of team*: Is there an appropriate number of people?
- ☐ *Team members*: Are the right people working together? Is there a need for sub-groups to be formed?
- ☐ *Team spirit*: Do I look for opportunities for building teamwork into jobs? Do methods of pay and bonus help to develop team spirit?
- ☐ *Discipline*: Are the rules seen to be reasonable? Am I fair and impartial in enforcing them?
- ☐ *Grievances*: Are grievances dealt with promptly? Do I take action on matters that are likely to disrupt the group?
- ☐ *Consultation*: Is this genuine? Do I encourage and welcome ideas and suggestions?
- ☐ *Briefing:* Is this regular? Does it cover current plans, progress and future developments?
- ☐ *Representation*: Am I prepared to represent the feelings or views of the group when required?
- ☐ *Support*: Do I visit people at their work when the team is apart? Do I then represent to the individual the whole team in my manner and encouragement?

Idea 25: Developing the individual

Go through each heading and question below. If the answers to any are unsatisfactory, draw up a plan to put each of them right. Some you can deal with today or tomorrow; for others you will need to plan ahead.

- ☐ *Targets*: Have they been agreed and as far as possible quantified?
- ☐ *Induction*: Does he/she really know the other team members and the organization?
- ☐ *Achievement*: Does he/she know how his/her work contributes to the overall result?
- ☐ *Responsibilities*: Has he/she got a clear and accurate job description? Can I delegate more to him/her?
- ☐ *Authority*: Does he/she have sufficient authority for his/her task?
- ☐ *Training*: Has adequate provision been made for training or retraining, both technical and as a team member?
- ☐ *Recognition*: Do I emphasize people's successes? In failure, is criticism constructive?
- ☐ *Growth*: Does he/she see the chance of development? Does he/she see some pattern of career?
- ☐ *Performance*: Is this regularly reviewed?
- ☐ *Reward*: Are work, capacity and pay in balance?
- ☐ *The task*: Is he/she in the right job? Has he/she the necessary resources?
- ☐ *The person*: Do I know this person well? What makes him/her different from others?
- ☐ *Time/attention*: Do I spend enough with individuals listening, developing, counselling?
- ☐ *Grievances*: Are these dealt with promptly?

- ☐ *Security*: Does he/she know about pensions, redundancy and so on?
- ☐ *Appraisal*: Is the overall performance of each individual regularly reviewed in face-to-face discussions?

The power of a team to accomplish its mission is directly related to how well the leader selects and develops the team members.

Idea 26: The individual and teams

As a leader you should be aware of and develop a clear understanding of the following areas:

1. Team properties:
   - Common background/history (or lack of it).
   - Participation patterns.
   - Communication.
   - Cohesiveness.
   - Atmosphere.
   - Standards.
   - Structure.
   - Organization.
   - Changes over time (forming, storming, norming and performing), both progressive and regressive.
   - How to change team properties if the evidence calls for change.
2. Team roles being defined, but with room left for individual personality.
3. Team member functions:
   - Distinction between *content* (*what* is said and done) and *process* (*how* it is said and done) in group functioning.
   - Difference between behaviour related to the *task*, behaviour related to *maintenance* of the team and behaviour that expresses individual *idiosyncrasies*.
   - Team leader functions (as above).
4. The individual:
   - Balancing the interests and self-expression of individuals and the wider interests of the team.
   - How the value of the task draws individuals/team together.

- How having sound values motivates individuals in teams.

5 Team processes:

- See what is really going on.
- Note that improved decision making rests on seeing beneath the surface the pressures that influence the team.
- The calmness of the leader creates calmness and interdependence within the team.
- Avoid team flight into abstractions.
- Aim for consensus (only where possible).
- Assess team view of authority to see how processes/ decisions are being affected by it.

6 Teams within teams:

- Be aware of teams within teams and act accordingly to regain cohesiveness or sub-divide the team.
- Watch out for hostility, communication failure and mistrust as signs of team fragmentation.
- Develop teamwork between teams as well as within them.
- Appreciate that winning can be as destructive to teams as losing, if not worse, unless both outcomes are handled well.

Idea 27: From good to great – hallmarks of a high-performance team

> *When people are of one mind and heart they can have Mount Tai (a famous mountain in Shandon Province – the highest known to Confucius).*
>
> Chinese proverb

Effective leadership has an end-product: the high-performance team. Its characteristics are described below.

Clear, realistic and challenging objectives

The team is focused on what has to be done – broken down into stretching but feasible goals, both team and individual. Everyone knows what is expected of him or her.

Shared sense of purpose

This doesn't mean that the team can recite the mission statement in unison! Purpose here is energy plus direction – what engineers call a vector. It should animate and invigorate the whole team. All share a sense of ownership and responsibility for team success.

Best use of resources

A high-performance team ensures that resources are allocated for strategic reasons for the good of the whole. They are not seen as the private property of the individual team member or of any part of the organization. Resources here include people and their time, not just money, buildings, equipment and other material assets.

Progress review

The best teams are eager to monitor their own performance, generating practical ideas for incremental improvements. These improvements encompass *process* – *how* we work together – as well as *content* (or task) – *what* we do together.

Building on experience

A blame culture mars any team. Errors will be made, but the greatest error of all is to do nothing so as to avoid making any! A wise team learns from failure, realizing that success is a poor teacher and that continual success may well breed complacency and even arrogance.

Mutual trust and support

A good team trusts its members to pursue their part in the common task. Appreciation is expressed and recognition given. People play to each other's strengths and cover each other's weaknesses. The level of mutual support is high. The atmosphere is one of openness and trust.

Communication

People listen to one another and build on one another's contributions. They communicate openly, freely and with skill (clearly, concisely, simply and with tact). Issues, problems and weaknesses are not sidestepped. Differences of opinion are respected. Team members know when to be very supportive and sensitive, and when to challenge and be intellectually tough.

Riding out the storms

In times of turbulent change it is never going to be all plain sailing. When unavoidable storms and crises arise, an excellent team rises to the challenge and demonstrates its sterling worth. It has resilience.

How does my team measure up against these benchmarks? (Give it a mark out of 10 for each benchmark.)
What actions do I need to take to help my team reach the 80 points level?

Sixteen Greatest Ideas for Getting the Best from Your Team

Idea 28: The 50:50 rule of motivation

Although I discuss their ideas in this section, I have come to the conclusion that Maslow, Herzberg and that school of thought are only half right about motivation. Fifty percent of our motivation comes from within us as we respond to our internal program of needs; fifty percent comes from outside ourselves, especially from the leadership we encounter in life.

My '50:50 rule', as it has become known, is not meant to be mathematically accurate; rather, it is indicative of the ever-shifting balance between internal and external influences. From it I have deduced a set of practical rules (see Idea 29) for leaders who want to motivate others. They will enable you to put other theories of motivation into perspective. The important thing is to apply these principles, for they connect up with the other fifty percent of motivators – the internal sets of needs and values that is in all of us.

'As a leader, make sure that you get your fifty percent right by practicing these principles before you criticize others for being under-motivated.'

Idea 29: Eight rules for motivating people

1 Be motivated yourself.
2 Select people who are highly motivated.
3 Treat each person as an individual.
4 Set realistic and challenging targets.
5 Remember that progress motivates.
6 Create a motivating environment.
7 Provide fair rewards.
8 Give recognition.

Have I moved on yet from the 'carrot-and-stick', reward-and-fear approach to motivation?

If you apply these eight rules you will find that you are becoming an inspiring leader. For you will be already going far beyond trying to move people by financial incentives or appeals to fear, those levels that the old-style bosses of yesteryear used to the exclusion of all else. You will be imparting to others your own spirit.

One of the most inspiring leaders of our time is Nelson Mandela. He was named after the famous British naval hero of that name. When he was still a young captain, Horatio Nelson received a letter from Admiral Lord St Vincent that included the words:

> *I never saw a man in our profession who possessed the magic art of infusing the same spirit into others which inspired their own actions as you do. All agree there is but one Nelson.*

Idea 30: Maslow's hierarchy of needs

If you know the nature of water it is easier to row a boat.

Chinese proverb

A sketch map of individual needs – which is useful for managers when considering individuals – can be drawn from Maslow's hierarchy of needs (first developed in 1954). Nevertheless, you should remember that his theory does not fully appreciate individual differences or the fact that each person has a unique set of needs and values.

Maslow identified five motivating factors in his hierarchy of needs and indicated that as each need is satisfied, others then emerge. He identified:

1. Physiological needs (including hunger, thirst, sleep).
2. Safety needs (security and protection from danger).
3. Social needs (belonging, acceptance, social life, friendship and love).
4. Self-esteem (self-respect, achievement, status, recognition).
5. Self-actualization (growth, accomplishment, personal development).

However, bear the following points in mind:

- Individuals do not necessarily move up the hierarchy on the principle that a 'satisfied need ceases to motivate', although that can be the case.
- Different levels of needs can kick in at random points on the scale toward the full satisfaction of needs.
- Culture, age and other factors can affect the importance of different needs to different people and at different stages in their lives.

- Satisfying some needs can be sacrificed in order to try to satisfy higher-level needs.

Use Maslow's needs as a sketch map – no more – of individual needs. As a leader, consider them in relation to each member of your team.

Idea 31: McGregor's Theory X and Theory Y

In *The Human Side of Enterprise* (1960), McGregor demonstrated that the way in which managers manage depends on the assumptions they make about human behaviour. He famously grouped these assumptions into Theory X and Theory Y.

Theory X: The traditional view of direction and control

- The average human being has an inherent dislike of work and will avoid it if possible.
- Because of this dislike of work, most people must be coerced, controlled, directed, and threatened with punishment to get them to give adequate effort toward the achievement of organizational objectives.
- The average human being prefers to be directed, wishes to avoid responsibility, has relatively little ambition and wants security above everything.

Theory Y: The integration of individual and organizational goals

- The expenditure of physical and mental effort in work is as natural as play or rest.
- External control and the threat of punishment are not the only means for bringing about effort toward organizational objectives. People will exercise self-direction and self-control in the service of objectives to which they are committed.
- Commitment to objectives is a function of the rewards associated with their achievement.
- The average human being learns, under proper conditions, not only to accept, but to seek responsibility.

- The capacity to exercise a relatively high degree of imagination, ingenuity and creativity in the solution of organizational problems is widely, not narrowly, distributed in the population.
- Under the conditions of modern industrial life, the intellectual potentialities of the average human being are only partially utilized.

McGregor drew on Maslow's work for much of Theory Y and put forward the cluster of features as an unproven hypothesis. Further research was needed to seek to prove it correct, which was conducted by Herzberg (see Idea 32).

In terms of management practice, Theory Y does reveal that in any individual within an organization there are untapped resources of goodwill, energy, creativity and intelligence.

What do I believe about human nature? Do I see people as a whole as inherently good or intrinsically bad?

Idea 32: Herzberg's motivation-hygiene theory

In Herzberg's research (published in his 1959 book *The Motivation to Work*), 14 factors were identified as the sources of good or bad feelings:

1. Recognition.
2. Achievement.
3. Possibility of growth.
4. Advancement.
5. Salary.
6. Interpersonal relations.
7. Supervision – technical.
8. Responsibility.
9. Company policy and administration.
10. Working conditions.
11. Work itself.
12. Factors in personal life.
13. Status.
14. Job security.

The eight *hygiene factors,* the ones that, according to Herzberg, can create *dissatisfaction* but have little or no power to create *job satisfaction,* are:

1. *Company policy and administration*: availability of clearly defined policies, especially those relating to people; adequacy of organization and management.
2. *Supervision*: technical; accessibility, competence and fairness of your superior.
3. *Interpersonal relations*: relations with supervisors, subordinates and colleagues; quality of social life at work.

4 *Salary*: total compensation package, such as wages, salary, pension, company car and other financially related benefits.
5 *Status*: position or rank in relation to others, symbolized by title, size of office or other tangible elements.
6 *Job security*: freedom from insecurity, such as loss of position or loss of employment altogether.
7 *Personal life*: the effect of work on family life, e.g. stress, unsocial hours or moving house.
8 *Working conditions*: the physical conditions in which you work; the amount of work; facilities available; and environmental aspects, e.g. ventilation, light, space, tools, noise.

The six *motivating factors* that lead to job *satisfaction* were identified by Herzberg as being:

1 *Achievement*: specific successes, such as the successful completion of a job, solutions to problems, vindication and seeing the results of your work.
2 *Recognition*: any act of recognition, whether notice or praise (separating recognition and reward from recognition with no reward).
3 *Possibility of growth*: changes in job where the potential for professional growth is increased.
4 *Advancement*: changes that enhance position or status at work.
5 *Responsibility*: being given real responsibility, matched with the necessary authority to discharge it.
6 *The work itself*: the actual job or phases of it.

The hygiene factors are those where people seek to avoid particular situations, whereas the motivating factors are matched with people's needs to achieve self-actualization or self-realization.

Giving priority to Herzberg's motivators and avoiding problems with the hygiene factors can help you as a manager to improve performance and give individuals greater job satisfaction.

How do Maslow, McGregor and Herzberg work for my team members *and* how do they work for *me*?

Idea 33: Manager's motivating checklist

There are five key elements that you should keep under continual review if you want to ensure that individuals stay motivated:

1. A sense of achievement in the job and the feeling that they are making a worthwhile contribution to the objectives of the team.
2. Jobs that are challenging and demanding, with responsibilities to match capabilities.
3. Adequate recognition for achievements.
4. Control over delegated duties.
5. A feeling that they are continuing to grow in experience and ability.

Achievement, recognition, work itself, responsibility and advancement – all add up to the growth (self-actualization) dimension of a job.

Idea 34: Ten ways to strengthen your own motivation

To motivate others successfully you have to feel highly motivated yourself. Here are ten ways to help you do just that:

1. Feel and act enthusiastically and in a committed way in your daily work.
2. Take responsibility when things go wrong rather than blaming others.
3. Identify ways in which you can lead by example.
4. Act according to the 50:50 principle: 50 percent of motivation comes from within ourselves, 50 percent from outside.
5. Motivate by work and example rather than manipulation.
6. Set an example naturally rather than in a calculated way.
7. Don't give up too easily.
8. Ensure you are in the right job for your own abilities, interests and temperament.
9. Be able to cite experience where what you have said or done has had an inspirational effect on individuals, the team or the organization.
10. Remember always that three badges of leadership are enthusiasm, commitment and perseverance.

How many of the above reflect my actions in the last week?

Idea 35: The seven indicators of high motivation

Here are seven signs that you may discern in yourself or others when motivation is high:

1. *Energy* – not necessarily being extrovert, but alertness and quiet resolve.
2. *Commitment* – to the common purpose.
3. *Staying power* – in the face of problems/difficulties/setbacks.
4. *Skill* – possession of skills indicates purpose and ambition.
5. *Single-mindedness* – energy applied in a single direction.
6. *Enjoyment* – goes hand in hand with motivation.
7. *Responsibility* – willingness to seek and accept it.

One practical way of using this list is to turn it into a set of benchmarks to assess the motivation and level of morale of your team at any given time.

Idea 36: Choosing people with motivation – the Michelangelo motive

Choosing people well means looking at motivation, ability and personality. When interviewing, look for evidence of the reality behind the interviewee's appearance and façade. If you do make a mistake, confront it and remedy the situation as early as you can.

The Italian Renaissance artist Michelangelo was once asked: 'Why did you take so much trouble painting those parts of the Sistine Chapel's roof that are invisible from below? No one will see them.' Michelangelo replied: 'God will.'

Looking for the 'Michelangelo motive' – where the quality of the work itself is a key motivator – can yield good results in selecting highly motivated individuals.

You should look for:

- A sense of pride in the individual's own work.
- Attention to detail.
- A willingness to 'walk the extra mile' to get things right.
- A total lack of the 'it's good enough, let it go' mentality.
- Inner direction or responsibility for the work (without the need for supervision).
- The ability to assess and evaluate his or her own work, independently of the opinions of others.

It should be stressed that perfectionism is not what is called for. What you are after is excellence, not perfection.

Managers should check whether individuals are in the right job with the right skills and abilities, otherwise motivation techniques will fail.

The aim is to select people who are naturally motivated: the right person for the right job.

'Select people who are already motivated.'

Idea 37: The key to motivating – treat each person as an individual

Find out what motivates the individuals in your team, do not rely on generalized theories or assumptions. You need to ask questions of each individual person and listen to their answers (there is more on listening skills in Ideas 82 and 83). Enter into a dialogue with each team member. Help them to clarify what it is that motivates them and use what you find to your mutual benefit.

In each person you should engender a sense of:

- Trust.
- Autonomy.
- Initiative.
- Industry.
- Integrity.
- Security.

Take time with each individual to:

- Encourage.
- Hearten.
- Inspire.
- Support.
- Embolden.
- Stimulate.

> *'To motivate others, you must be motivated yourself.'*

Idea 38: Using Jacob's ladder to set realistic and challenging targets

Setting realistic objectives or targets and defining the tasks to be achieved can only be done in the context of a good understanding of the organization's purpose and aims.

In the Bible there is a story of Jacob falling asleep and having a vision of a ladder set up between Earth and Heaven, with angels – the messengers of God – moving both downward and upward. So a 'Jacob's Ladder' links down-to-earth objectives and practical steps with higher aims and the more general or abstract purpose – it's two-way traffic, as you can see in the diagram.

Moving down the ladder, you are answering the question: '*How* are we going to achieve the common purpose?' The answer is by breaking down the purpose into the main aims, and the main aims in turn into more specific objectives or goals.

Moving up the ladder, you are seeking to answer the question: '*Why* are we doing this?' The answer to that question is that we are trying

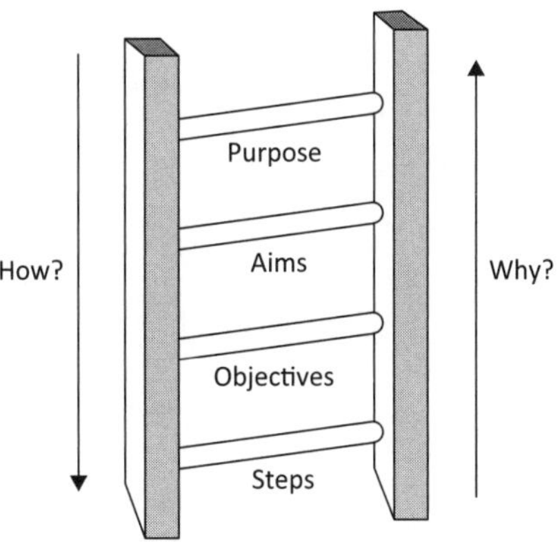

to achieve this objective in order to achieve this aim and satisfy this purpose.

Compare this forward-looking way of answering the question *why* with the backward-looking one: 'Because that's the way we've always done it.'

The targets you set (for short-term objectives or longer-term goals) should be:

- Specific.
- Clear.
- Time-bounded.

An objective or target must be realistic (feasible) and challenging. If you aim for the best you can often get It.

Targets must be agreed and monitored, with further action also agreed to maintain motivation toward the shared aims and objectives.

Idea 39: Giving feedback to reinforce and motivate

Feedback on progress (or even a relative lack of it) helps with motivation, either to spur people on, or to concentrate the mind on what still needs to be done.

Feedback is not given at all or sometimes not often enough, and people claim that's for these reasons:

- 'People don't need to be told how they are doing, they already know.'
- 'People take it easy if you say things are going well.'
- 'They are unhappy and cause trouble if you say things are not going well.'
- 'We lack the skills or the time to do it.'

And when you do give feedback, it needs to be the right kind. Feedback that is affirmative – praise – must be:

- Accurate.
- Sincere.
- Generous.
- Spontaneous.
- Fair.

Then it becomes true that, as the proverb says, 'Our praises are our wages'.

In contrast, praise must not be:

- Too much or too fulsome.
- Patronizing.
- Superior/condescending.

- Grudging.
- Calculated for effect.
- Unjustly bestowed.

Maintaining motivation depends on combining the act of informing with being inspiring. The rule is always to establish the truth first, before you attempt to encourage or inspire.

Be sparing in praise and more so in blame.

As industrialist Andrew Carnegie said to one of his plant bosses:

> *Don't tell me that the man is doing good work, tell me what good work he is doing.*

Idea 40: Maintaining morale to maintain motivation

Maintaining high morale is key to high motivation. Morale covers both the individuals separately and the team as a whole. Where an individual has low morale, the issues have to be addressed on an individual basis, but where group or team morale is low, the answer lies in diagnosing whether or not there is a lack of confidence in:

- Ultimate success.
- Current plan(s).
- Leadership/management.
- The capability of the team or organization.

Morale is basically the group's or individual's attitude to the common task, their confidence in the ultimate possibility of success and their consequent sense of purpose and collective energy.

It can be necessary to remotivate the team by rebuilding its self-confidence. You can do this by:

- Revisiting purpose – *why* is this important and worthwhile?
- Clarifying objectives.
- Reviewing the plans and resources needed.
- Demonstrating that success is within your grasp.
- Training for higher performance.
- Involving the team and individuals in key decisions.

Is individual and/or team morale high or low? What action should I and other leaders take to keep it high or to raise it if it's low?

Idea 41: Creating a motivating environment

Make sure that you create as motivating an environment as you can by observing these nine key points:

1. Beware of the insidious growth of a restrictive organization, one with a negative ethos and with a bureaucratic over-emphasis on controls.
2. Avoid public criticism of individuals.
3. Ensure that Herzberg's hygiene factors are catered for – the physical and psychological well-being of people should have a high priority.
4. Control systems should only be introduced where necessary and kept to a minimum.
5. Give people an input into decisions that affect their working lives (especially in respect of substantial change).
6. Keep units and sub-units as small as possible (larger units have a greater tendency to be bureaucratic and demotivational unless they have inspired leaders).
7. Pay attention to job design – avoid repetitive work, introduce variety.
8. Give people autonomy and a job with a 'product' that an individual can recognize as his/her own.
9. Ensure that each individual understands the significance of his/her job in relation to the whole, which will also encourage new ideas an innovation.

Idea 42: Giving fair rewards to the motivated

Although it is difficult to ensure that the financial reward an individual receives is fair (commensurate with contribution), effort must be applied in trying to get it right. There are other motivating 'returns' that individuals look for from jobs (as in Maslow's hierarchy of needs), but money is the one that has the main strategic importance for most people.

Most individuals like the combination of a fixed salary with a variable element related to performance or profits. Also of tactical importance are incentives to improve performance in key areas, such as sales, customer service and credit control.

Incentives can be in the form of cash, vouchers, merchandise or travel, but care must be taken to administer any incentive schemes fairly and without risking demotivating any 'losers'.

In providing fair rewards, the organization should ask itself:

- Do we have a scheme whereby financial reward is made up of a fixed and a variable element?
- Do we link performance and pay?
- Have we addressed the problems of whether to pay performance-related elements to the team or the individual?
- Do we actively consider changing our information systems to improve methods of rewarding performance?
- Do we have incentive schemes other than for sales people?
- Does our organization reward the behaviour/performance that it professes to value most highly?

- Do senior managers betray their lack of leadership by taking pay rises/bonuses when they expect others to do without them?

It is always worth remembering Herzberg's insight that salary has more power to make people dissatisfied or unhappy than it has power to motivate them.

Idea 43: Giving recognition to the motivated

Financial reward is seen by the recipient as a tangible form of recognition. There are other ways in which appreciation is expressed for what has been contributed. Recognition should be formal or informal, for the individual and/or the team, as appropriate.

If recognition is not given, an individual can feel unnoticed, unvalued and unrewarded. This leads to a drop in motivation and energy levels.

When giving recognition, you should try to ensure that you:

- Treat everyone in a fair and equal way.
- Reward real achievements or contributions.
- Reflect the core values of the organization.
- Use recognition to guide and encourage all concerned.
- Give recognition in public if possible.
- Give it formally and informally.
- Give it genuinely and sincerely.

It is a good idea to back up words of praise or recognition with some tangible gift. Other than financial payments, any words of recognition could be reinforced by giving:

- Time off (with pay).
- Tickets for an event or dinner out.
- A small gift.
- A special project of importance.
- A change in job title.

Find out what is going on, share praise that is received with subordinates, and say thank-you more often, because people really value positive recognition and are motivated by it.

Recognition is the oxygen of the human spirit.

Follow-up test

Teambuilding

- ☐ Have you applied the task, team and individual approach in leading your team?
- ☐ Have you agreed with your team members their main targets and continuing responsibilities, together with standards of performance, so that you can all recognize achievement?
- ☐ Do you recognize the contribution of each member of the team and encourage other team members to do the same?
- ☐ Have you set – and maintained – positive group norms or standards?
- ☐ In the event of success, do you acknowledge it and build on it? In the event of setbacks, do you identify what went well and give constructive guidance for improving future performance?
- ☐ How does your team rate against the criteria for a high-performance team?

Getting the best from your team

- ☐ Do you consciously try to motivate people by understanding their needs and aspirations?
- ☐ Are you motivated?
- ☐ Do you feel that you are getting the best from people?

- ☐ Are targets set and monitored, with feedback being clearly given?
- ☐ Do you show to those who work with you that you trust them by, for example, not hedging them around with unnecessary controls?
- ☐ Are there adequate opportunities for training and (where necessary) retraining?
- ☐ Do you encourage each individual to develop his or her capacities to the full?
- ☐ Is each individual's overall performance regularly reviewed in face-to-face discussions?
- ☐ Does financial reward match contribution?
- ☐ Do you make sufficient time to talk and listen, so that you understand the unique (and changing) profile of needs and wants in each person, enabling you to work with the grain of nature rather than against it?
- ☐ Out of the eight principles of motivation, which is the one that you need to give much more attention to?

'Be sparing with praise but liberal with thanks.'

PART FOUR

Thinking as a Leader

This section of the book looks first at decision making, an essential skill for you as a leader. It then examines ways in which you can generate new ideas yourself, stimulate a creative approach in your team, and build a truly innovative organization.

The intellectual side of leadership – effective practical thinking in all its applied forms – is so often neglected in the literature on the subject. But it's no use leading people in the wrong direction because you made the wrong decision.

You don't want to become a *misleader*. Making the right choices, exercising good judgment and having the skill to solve problems when they arise – people look for these abilities in their leaders. Like all other aspects of leadership, there is a global body of knowledge concerning them which I can share with you in Part Four.

Listening to suggestions and ideas, being open to persuasion before a decision is taken and then being decisive yourself, all these important leadership skills are learnable.

Part Four also includes an introduction to creativity and innovation. As a leader you need to know how to generate new ideas. Ideas are the seeds of change, positive and desirable change in your business.

Your leadership challenge is to release the creativity that is latent in your team or organization, and to turn it into improvement and progress, leading to better services and products today and new ones tomorrow. To lead is always to do new things.

Twelve Greatest Ideas for Decision Making

Idea 44: Refining your decision-making skills

You need to be able to choose the action or course of action that is the best for you and your organization to meet its objective(s). An effective decision is one that produces the goods; that is, it gives the desired end result.

It is important to be able to project ahead, to take the expected and unexpected into account, to have contingency plans in case events intrude in such a way to turn a good decision into a bad one.

There are usually several different decisions that can be taken and pressure to decide. Decide you must, though, even if trial and error are then used to assess the decision, amend it or overturn it.

Fear of failure must not serve to make you risk averse. Rather, it should push you harder to 'think until it hurts'.

An effective decision has these six elements:

1. Defining the objective.
2. Gathering sufficient information.
3. Identifying the feasible options.
4. Evaluating those options.
5. Making the decision (choosing an option).
6. Testing its implementation: by feel, by measurement and by assessment.

You should also listen to your 'feel-right?' test – do warning lights flash or alarm bells sound? If so, rework decision elements 1–6. Your own experience or that of others helps to develop your 'feel' for decisions.

A decision is only effective if it is implemented – and that means getting the desired results through people. For that, other people

need to be included in the decision-making process. You need to develop your skills in appreciating when it is most appropriate to include others and when you have to make the decision on your own.

With all decisions there are three parts to the story: making the decision, implementing it, and living with the consequences.

Idea 45: The decision maker as effective thinker

An effective decision maker is always an effective and clear thinker. The three essential skills are those of:

1 Analyzing.
2 Synthesizing.
3 Valuing.

An effective decision maker knows that quick decisions are not necessarily the best ones, and that true decisiveness only results from thinking things through. Key decisions (and recognizing when you are being asked to make or be involved in the making of key decisions) demand that great care go into analyzing (the component elements), synthesizing (putting ideas together) and valuing (assessing relative worth).

The crucial elements in decision making are:

- Establishing the facts.
- Considering the options.
- Deciding the course of action.

In order to achieve these elements, the truly effective thinker has these attributes:

- Skills of analysis, synthesis and valuing.
- Being open to intuition.
- Imagination (to find new ways to overcome problems).
- Creativity (coupled with careful preliminary work).
- Being receptive to new ideas.

- Humility – recognizing when others may have better powers or knowledge and combining with their thinking with your own.

'This problem is an opportunity in disguise.'

Always operate in the context of facing reality and of seeking for and speaking the truth.

To improve your performance you need to ask yourself honestly how good your skills are (and have been) at:

- Decision making.
- Problem solving.
- Creative thinking.

Do I make false assumptions and jump to conclusions? Am I prone to faulty reasoning or not listening to others?

Idea 46: The manager as decision maker

Management is about 'deciding what to do and getting it done'.

Success in business stems from good-quality management decisions first of all and then effectiveness in implementation, which depends on the skills of leadership, influencing, communication and motivation.

One survey of 200 leaders of industry and commerce ranked 'the ability to take decisions' as the most important attribute of top management.

The logical or rational manager will invariably follow this decision-making model (see the diagram):

- Define objective.
- Collect information.
- Develop options.
- Evaluate and decide.
- Implement.
- Monitor consequences.
- Sense effects.

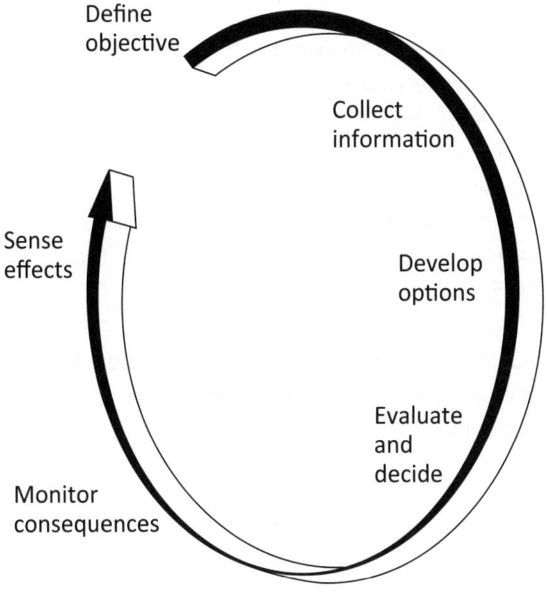
Define
objective
Collect
information
Develop
options
Evaluate
and
decide
Monitor
consequences
Sense
effects

Idea 47: How to avoid the trap of bad compromise decisions

US research into decisions by public-sector officials suggests that decision makers rarely settle for the 'best' or optimum solution, being affected by emotion, power, politics, the influences of other people and our own values. Often a decision is a bad compromise between different courses of action, one that:

- Agrees to some extent with your own personal interests, needs or values.
- Meets the value standards of superiors.
- Is acceptable to those affected (by the decision and involved in carrying it out).
- Looks reasonable.
- Has an escape element of self-justification if it all goes wrong.

Clearly, such an approach to decision making must be far removed from your own approach! Follow the ideas in this section to make sure you do better.

Idea 48: How to use analysis in decision making

An essential part of analysis is to be able to break the whole up into its component parts, particularly splitting complex matters into more simple elements.

The hallmarks of an analytical mind are that it:

- Establishes the relationship between the parts and the whole.
- Finds the root cause(s) of the problem.
- Identifies the issue(s) at stake, the 'either/or' on which a decision rests.

Analytical ability is improved by:

- Working from first principles.
- Establishing the facts and separating them from opinions, assumptions or suppositions.
- Asking yourself questions (as in 'When did the problem first arise?' as well as our six friends Who, What, Why, When, Where and How?).
- Continually checking the premise and/or the steps in logic, a fault in which can undermine good reasoning.
- Thinking backwards from the desired outcome to potential solutions.
- Organizing the facts.
- Seeing the problem as a solution in disguise.

Analysis is not, however, an end in itself and trying to over-analyze can lead to inactivity or 'paralysis by analysis', as it has been called.

What evidence do I have that others regard me as a clear thinker?

Idea 49: The role of synthesis – a holistic approach – in decision making

Decision making requires you to 'take a view' and that depends on the ability to combine parts or elements to form a whole: synthesis. Holistic is a useful word to use in this regard, as it also conveys the approach, especially in business, which recognizes that 'wholes' are produced by grouping various units together, where it is difficult to analyze them in their parts without losing this wholeness. Hence a holistic view needs to be taken in business decision making.

One difficulty is that analysis can be the enemy of synthesis and vice versa. There is a need in business to be able to see the wood for the trees (holism) rather than only the trees (analysis).

In this sense, and in business too, the whole is greater than the sum of its parts. Business thinking is a good example of the Gestalt approach, whereby we arrive at an understanding of:

- The overall significance rather than a mechanistic explanation.
- The relationships between events, not just the events themselves. Events do not occur in isolation, only in a setting that gives each event significance.

Managers need to take this whole view – not see things as a marketing problem, or a production issue, or a stock control difficulty, or a people problem, or a management failure. Look at the whole to see what that can yield by way of a solution.

Integrating facts, ideas and opinions is like the ability to synthesize, and strengthens the manager's decision making. Particularly in assessing financial performance, a manager needs to view the figures as a whole as well as in detail.

Dust as we are, the immortal spirit grows
Like harmony in music; there is a dark
Inscrutable workmanship that reconciles
Discordant elements, makes them cling together
In one society.

William Wordsworth

Idea 50 – The role of imagination in decision making

An important attribute to have in business is the skill to visualize the whole in your imagination. It is part and parcel of being creative in your approach to decision making. Being imaginative is a crucial ability to develop in yourself and others: it helps to surprise the competition, to exploit the unexpected, to invent new products or services, or to solve problems creatively.

Indicators of a healthy level of imagination are the abilities to:

- Recall events easily and visually.
- Foresee what may happen before an event.
- Be inventive or creative artistically, mechanically or verbally.
- Daydream about future desirable events.

These elements of recall, visualizing, creating, foreseeing and fantasizing contribute to effective thinking in business as much as in the arts or scientific fields.

> *'One of the greatest creative satisfactions in life is to be told that it's impossible – and then to do it!'*

Idea 51: The role of conceptual thinking in decision making

Although a concept may appear to be an abstraction arrived at by analysis, it has a different feel because:

- It is a whole (and as such more than the sum of its parts).
- It is a developing entity in its own right.

A concept is 'something conceived in the mind'. Conceptual thinking in business addresses such issues as:

- What business are we in?
- What are its strengths/weaknesses?
- What are its purposes/aims?

Conceptual thinking should be kept separate from decision making, even though decisions are made on the basis of the concepts that we have developed.

Concepts can be used in 'profiling' business development, but they then have to be made more specific in the form of proposals or plans before being implemented. Concepts can be a way of taking your mind away from the particular and include ideas about what *ought* to be as opposed to what *is*.

Good-quality concepts will underpin good-quality business decisions. Therefore you should generate clear, well-defined concepts and develop them.

Idea 52: The role of intuition in decision making

It is too easy to be dismissive of intuition, the ability to 'sense' what needs to be done or to 'smell' trouble and opportunities alike. In fact, it is an invaluable key to making and taking effective decisions.

It is not always possible to analyze problems into solutions, and intuition is the useful power to know what has happened or what to do. Interestingly, the powers of intuition are diminished by stress and general fatigue, so your ability to be insightful in decision making can be adversely affected by these factors.

'Intuition', 'instinct', 'first impressions', 'feel', 'hunch' and 'flair' are important dimensions to explore not only when faced with decision making, but also when considering business activities and the systems to run them.

Idea 53: The role of originality and innovation in decision making

Creative and innovative thinking can help in making decisions that develop a business in new directions, so they are elements to encourage in yourself and others.

Be prepared to work at problems or issues to encourage creativity or insight to come into play. Be prepared also to encourage new ideas by rewarding those who put them forward, and to try out and innovate new products and services as well as new ways of doing things.

There are more ideas for creativity and innovation later in Part Four.

> *'Always try to turn a disadvantage into an advantage.'*

Idea 54: The concept of value in decision making

Along with analysis and synthesis, valuing is the third essential element of effective thinking and decision making.

As we have seen, the ability to make decisions has two main aspects:

1 Establishing the truth or the true facts.
2 Knowing what to do.

You must take time over the first aspect, otherwise integrity – or adherence to the value of truth – is lost in the process. Thinking first and then deciding what to do is the correct order in decision making. Getting at the truth should make it easier to know what to do.

In many respects, it is better to behave as if truth is an object, something that must be discovered. The truth, and valuing what one discovers, should be seen as 'objective', with your own views and conditioning recognized and relied on or discounted as needs be.

When you rely on others, as managers so often do, you may have to sift information from their 'valuations' (information plus judgment). This is another form of valuing – of knowing who and when to trust to give you the truth, or the truth backed by acceptable value judgments.

Questioning is a valid part of establishing the credentials of the adviser and the credibility of the advice. Can you trust this person to tell the truth backed by sufficient expertise or insight? You will learn by experience to recognize the people who:

- Tell you what they think you want to hear.
- Express a view that they think might agree with your own.

- Are watching their backs.
- Try to hide things.

Be scrupulous in establishing the truth – ask questions until you are satisfied that you have it right.

You are good at valuing if you can say that invariably you have good judgment; the converse is also true. Knowing the truth or reality can then be followed by deciding what to do.

Also, beware of inaccurate figures (even from accounts departments!), faulty statistics, errors in facts, hidden assumptions and specious assurances – everything must be tested for accuracy and truth.

> *'Truth is what corresponds to reality. It is the only sure foundation for decisions that endure.'*

Idea 55: How to weigh up the options in decision making

> *If your enemy has two options open to him, be sure that he will choose the third.*
>
> Bismarck

It is invariably necessary to choose a particular course of action out of a range of possible options. What is the best way of ensuring that your own selection process is a sound one?

The basic point here is that you should never assume that there is only one option open to you. Consider a number of options (or as many sensible and pertinent ones as you can muster), many of which will be directly dictated or affected by the facts that you can establish. Gathering information also helps you to collect options, and even to consider options that you might think are closed to you (e.g. increasing price, scrapping low-profit items etc.).

Selecting and working through a range of options means considering the following:

- Which options are possible?
- Which of those are feasible?
- How can feasible options be reduced to two choices, the 'either/or'?
- Which option (or a mixture of options) should be chosen?
- Is any action really necessary at all, now, later?
- Should options be kept open, so no choice is yet made?

Avoid feeling any compulsion to take action when opting to take no action would be better. Never assume that there are only two possibilities, at least until you have weighed up all the feasible ones you can within a reasonable time frame.

When considering the options beware of false assumptions: test all of them for validity.

At the same time, it is essential to understand the other factors that can limit the range and choice of options or their applicability. You need to exercise judgment about:

- Time.
- Information.
- Resources.
- Knowledge.

Again, beware of false assumptions – including about these factors. You have to know the real (not assumed) limits that the above factors can impose on the options available to you.

Generating more options, particularly if initially there seems to be only one, will usually lead to better decision making. This is where imagination, creative thinking and intuition can help.

Considering fresh possibilities and suspending judgment while generating them (through brainstorming) can increase the range of options by avoiding negativity. Don't fall prey to statements such as:

- 'It won't work.'
- 'We do it this way.'
- 'It can't be done.'
- 'It failed before.'

When weighing up the options you must refine your skills at considering the consequences, both the possible and the probable. This will lead to an assessment of risks and rewards. Both sets should be carefully calculated in a cost/benefit equation.

Can I accept the risk of failure? What is the worst that can happen if this option fails, and can I accept that?

Then use your judgment to select from the range of options that you have been carefully weighed and assessed as to their probable outcomes.

When facing a difficult decision, it could be worth getting people together, asking for ideas or brainstorming them, and testing and evaluating the suggestions.

Thirteen Greatest Ideas for Creativity and Innovation

Idea 56: Seven obstacles to creativity

There are a number of obstacles that inhibit creativity. The seven main ones are:

1 Negativity.
2 Fear of failure.
3 Lack of quality thinking time.
4 Over-conformance with rules and regulations.
5 Making assumptions.
6 Applying too much logic.
7 Thinking that you are not creative.

These obstacles can be seen in the following identikit profile of the non-creative person, someone who is:

- Not able to think positively about problems (and does not see them as opportunities).
- Too busy or stressed to think objectively or at all.
- Very self-critical.
- Timid in putting forward a new idea (fearing ridicule).
- Viewed as a conformist by friends or colleagues.
- Prone to apply logic as a first and last resort.
- Skeptical that many people are capable of being creative.
- Unable to think laterally.
- Uninspired even when confronted with a new idea.

On the other hand, creativity can be encouraged in people (including yourself) by exploring some of the qualities and characteristics of creative thinkers and the activities or steps that can be undertaken to improve the processes involved. This is what this section aims to do.

How many of the seven obstacles to creativity do I recognize in myself?
How am I going to overcome them?
Which are the easiest ones to deal with first?

Idea 57: Ten things a creative person ought to be

You *can* learn to be more creative. Here are some suggestions:

1. Think beyond the invisible frameworks that surround problems and situations.
2. Recognize when assumptions are being made and challenge them.
3. Spot blinkered thinking and widen the field of vision (to draw on the experiences of other individuals or businesses).
4. Develop and adapt ideas from more than one source.
5. Practice serendipity (finding valuable and agreeable things when not particularly seeking them) – having a wide attention span and range of interests is important.
6. 'Transfer technology' from one field to another.
7. Be open and prepared to use chance or unpredictable things or events to your advantage.
8. Explore thought processes and the key elements of your mind at work in analyzing, valuing and synthesizing.
9. Use your 'depth' mind (the unconscious mind), for example by sleeping on a problem to generate creative solutions to problems.
10. Note down thoughts and ideas that apparently drop into your mind unsolicited so that they are not forgotten.

Discovery consists of seeing what everyone has seen and thinking what nobody has thought.

Idea 58: Seven ways to stimulate creativity

1 Use analogy to improve imaginative thinking – find models or solutions in nature, in existing products or services and/or in other organizations, so that you are not always 'reinventing the wheel'.
2 Try, as appropriate, sometimes to make the strange familiar and the familiar strange in order to spark new ideas.
3 Make connections with points that are:
   - Apparently irrelevant.
   - Disguised, buried or not easily accessible.
   - Outside your own sphere of expertise.
   - Lacking in authority.
4 Suspend judgment to encourage the creative process and avoid premature criticism – analysis and criticism repress creativity.
5 Know when to leave a problem for solutions to emerge – remain aware but detached. Patience is important here, as is the suspension of judgment.
6 Tolerate ambiguity and occasionally live with doubt and uncertainty.
7 Stimulate your own curiosity (in everything, including travel) and your skills of observation, listening, reading and recording.

'The most original person adapts from the most sources.'

Idea 59: The four main stages of creativity

The intellect has little to do on the road to discovery. There comes a leap in consciousness, call it intuition or what you will, and the solution comes to you and you don't know how or why.

Albert Einstein

- *Preparation* – the hard work. You have to collect and sort the relevant information, analyze the problem as thoroughly as you can, and explore possible solutions.
- *Incubation* – the depth mind phase. Mental work – analyzing, synthesizing and valuing – continues on the problem in your subconscious mind. The parts of the problem separate and new combinations occur. These may involve other ingredients stored away in your memory.
- *Insight* – the 'Eureka' moment. A new idea emerges into your conscious mind, either gradually or suddenly, like a fish flashing out of the water. These moments often occur when you are not thinking about the problem but are in a relaxed frame of mind.
- *Validation* – This is where your valuing faculty comes into play. A new idea, insight, intuition, hunch or solution needs to be thoroughly tested. This is especially so if it is to form the basis for action of any kind.

Although it is useful for you to have this framework in mind, remember that the actual mental process is a lot more untidy than the above list suggests.

Think of the phases as being four notes on a piano that can be played in different sequences or combined in complex chords.

Idea 60: The seven key players in innovation

It is worth identifying some of the key players who, if they were all present within an organization, would surely make it unbeatable.

1. *Creative thinker* – produces new and original ideas.
2. *Innovator* – brings new products/services to the market or changes existing ones.
3. *Inventor* – produces new and commercial ideas.
4. *Entrepreneur* – conceives of or receives ideas and translates them into business reality to exploit a market opportunity.
5. *Intrapreneur* – responsible for innovation within an organization.
6. *Champion* – determination and commitment to implement an idea.
7. *Sponsor* – backs an idea and helps remove obstacles.

Successful businesses run on positive change. Effective innovation requires:

- A blend of new ideas.
- The ability to get things done.
- Sound commercial sense.
- Customer focus.
- A conducive organizational climate.

Leaders should be able to:

- Lead on the journey of change.
- Encourage creativity in their teams.
- Provide an organizational environment in which innovation can thrive.

- Use a variety of techniques to stimulate ideas for products/services/systems and to generate ways of bringing them to fruition.

The management of innovation must be seen as a process with three phases:

1. The generation of ideas (from individuals and teams).
2. The harvesting of ideas (people evaluating ideas).
3. The implementation of ideas (teams developing and introducing ideas to the final, customer-satisfied stage).

> *'Creative thinking makes innovation possible – teamwork makes innovation happen.'*

Idea 61: How to recruit and retain creative people

You need creative people for jobs where they are appropriate. The characteristics of a creative person tend to be:

- High general intelligence.
- Strongly motivated.
- Stimulated by challenge.
- Vocational in attitude to work.
- Able to hold contradictory ideas together in creative tension.
- Curious, with good listening and observing skills.
- Able to think for themselves, independent in thought.
- Neither an introvert nor an extrovert, but rather in the middle.
- Interested in many areas/things.

Creative individuals thrive if they are:

- Appreciated and receive recognition.
- Given freedom to work in their area(s) of greatest interest.
- Allowed contact with stimulating colleagues.
- Given stimulating projects to work on.
- Free to make mistakes.

If you are to retain creative people, you should ensure not only that their creativity continues to thrive in the right environment, but also that financially they are flexibly and well rewarded and given the freedom to operate and work without being stifled by excess bureaucracy.

The quality of an innovative organization depends ultimately on the quality of the people you employ.

Idea 62: How to encourage creativity

It is not always easy to manage the creative and innovative aspects of teamwork. Ideally, individuals need to share the values, characteristics and interests of the other team members, to work with them in harmony and yet have something different to offer.

Belbin identified nine team-member roles, some of which are relatively self-explanatory:

1 Plant (solves difficult problems).
2 Resource manager.
3 Coordinator.
4 Shaper.
5 Monitor/evaluator.
6 Team worker (cooperative, diplomatic).
7 Implementer.
8 Completer.
9 Specialist.

A good team will exhibit all of the above 'roles', not necessarily with nine different people, but with fewer team members adopting different roles to complete the task.

Besides helping individuals to 'perform' the Belbin roles within a team, encouraging creativity in teams depends on a manager's skills in:

- Using the different skills within the team (having first identified the attributes of each individual).
- Ensuring that conflicts of ideas are allowed to happen and are tolerated by all.
- Recognizing particularly good contributions.

- Helping the team generate ideas (e.g. by brainstorming).
- Creating an open environment where individual team members can speak up honestly.

Idea 63: How communication can reinforce innovation

Feedback can maintain interest levels and providing information about progress made can stimulate further activity and more progress.

Good communication can help improve creativity and innovation and should:

- Stress the importance of new ideas and show how business has improved because of their implementation.
- Indicate why ideas have been rejected or accepted.
- Give progress reports on ideas originated by individuals or teams.
- Recognize and reward appropriately for successful innovation.

Do people know that I always listen to new ideas?

Idea 64: Overcoming obstacles to creativity and innovation

Too often good ideas wither on the vine and die. Don't let this happen to yours.

If you're not careful, creativity and innovation can be killed off by:

- An initial response of outright condemnation, ridicule, rejection, damning criticism or faint praise.
- The vested interest of a particular person or department.
- Too early an evaluation or judgement. Sometimes suspending judgment early on can see an idea grow and reach a strong stage where it will work.

Managers who are creative and act in innovation-friendly ways have not only the usual leadership skills (defining objectives, planning, controlling, supporting and reviewing in the areas of task, team and individual needs) but also are able to:

- Accept risk.
- Work with half-formed ideas.
- Bend the rules.
- Respond quickly.
- Be enthusiastic (to motivate others).

Do I try to look for the good in an idea rather than only seeing the bad?

Idea 65: Making your organization good at innovation

Your organization itself has to provide an environment in which creativity and innovation can flourish.

The five hallmarks of organizations that are good at innovation (and are not just paying lip service to it) are:

1. Top-level commitment.
2. Flexible in organizational structure.
3. Tolerant of failure (and not risk averse).
4. Encouraging of teamwork and innovation.
5. Good at open and constructive communication.

> *Managing innovation... [is a] challenge to management... especially top management, and a touchstone of its competence.*
>
> Peter Drucker

Organizations need to work at the main ingredients for success in managing innovation and apply themselves to the five hallmarks listed above.

Top-level commitment

This commitment must be visible and audible. Top management must ensure that any blocks to innovation are removed and that the presence of inhibiting bureaucracy or individuals does not foul up the process. Chief executives and senior managers must value new ideas and innovation and participate actively to ensure that everyone knows of their commitment to positive and useful change.

Sometimes the need for short-term profits can dull the edge of creativity and innovation. Only top management can prevent this happening – by taking the long-term not the short-term view.

Flexible in organizational structure

The antithesis of the innovative organization is the bureaucratic one. Weber's characteristics of bureaucratic organizations are as follows:

- Authority is impersonal and formal.
- A strong emphasis on functional specialization.
- A rule for every eventuality.
- A strong emphasis on hierarchy and status.
- Clearly laid down procedures (red tape).
- A proliferation of paperwork.
- Security of employment and advancement by seniority.

At the opposite end of the scale is the flexible organization, which is one:

- Capable of responding to changing situations.
- Where barriers between staff in different areas are minimized.
- With a flat rather than pyramid organizational structure.
- Where decision making is pushed downward to where the organization meets its customers or suppliers.
- With entrepreneurial flair present at all levels.
- With the ability to develop and test more than one solution to problems encountered.
- With efficient rather than stifling monitoring systems.
- With enough 'discipline' to get things done.
- With a balance between freedom and order.

Tolerant of failure

Innovation and risk go hand in hand. Management that goes into critical overdrive when mistakes occur (rather than analyzing them to learn from the failure) smothers creativity and innovation. Risks can yield failure, but not taking risks can spell total disaster and an end to profits and growth.

Unless failure results from negligence, recklessness or complete incompetence, managers should not seek out scapegoats or exact revenge. Profits are the reward for taking risks and innovative organizations learn to live with risk.

Encouraging teamwork and innovation

In innovation it can be said that none of us is as good as all of us. Teamwork and innovation are better in organizations where:

- The climate is open.
- Participation is encouraged.
- Facts and information are readily available.
- Change is managed positively.
- Resources are provided for training and development.
- Rules are at a minimum (with policies and guidelines instead).
- Internal communication is good and more by mouth than memo.
- Respect is given to all colleagues (but not on demand by management – it has to be earned).
- Managers are themselves highly motivated.
- Teamwork often transcends departmental boundaries.

Good at open and constructive communication

Communication should be good laterally and vertically (and flatter organizations should – in theory at least – encourage good lateral

communication). Should managers ensure a good flow of information, ideas can emerge as a result. Cross-fertilization can create more (and better) ideas, particularly where departmental, divisional boundaries are crossed.

> *'None of us is as good as all of us, so build a community of creativity and innovation.'*

Idea 66: Checklist for the innovative organization

- ☐ Is the top management team committed to innovation?
- ☐ Does the organization clearly express its vision (which should include an emphasis on innovation)?
- ☐ Is the chief executive openly enthusiastic for change?
- ☐ Are mutual stimulation, feedback and constructive criticism all at high levels of activity?
- ☐ Is the organization good at teamwork, including the use of project teams?
- ☐ Are mistakes and failures accepted as part of risk taking?
- ☐ Do creative people join and stay with the organization?
- ☐ Is innovation rewarded (financially or by promotion or both)?
- ☐ Are lateral communications good?
- ☐ Can ideas be exchanged informally and are opportunities provided to do this?
- ☐ Does the organization make excuses not to innovate?
- ☐ Are resources given to new ideas?
- ☐ Is the structure flexible?
- ☐ Is decision making pushed down to the lowest level at which decisions could be taken?
- ☐ Do all staff see themselves as part of the processes of creativity and innovation?
- ☐ Does the organization take a long-term view of the benefits of innovation?
- ☐ Is innovation part of the organization's vision and strategy?
- ☐ Is it fun to work in your organization?

Score your organization 'yes' or 'no'. If you have more than nine 'no' scores, it's not good!

If you take risks, you will make some mistakes, but if you do not take calculated risks, you are doomed to failure.

Idea 67: Ways to generate ideas in an organization

Do I operate an effective internal market for potentially innovative ideas in my organization?

It is interesting to note that organizations can get ideas from, among other sources:

- R&D (internal or external).
- Staff.
- Competitors.
- Suppliers.
- Customers.
- Quality circles.

One survey demonstrated that SMEs (small and medium-sized enterprises) can get ideas from, in order of importance:

1 Staff.
2 Customers.
3 Market and competition.
4 Board and planning group.
5 Sales department.
6 Suppliers.
7 Managing director.
8 Consultants.
9 Shows and exhibitions.

Ideas have to be sieved – by individuals or by teams – to choose and refine the best ideas to develop them and take to market.

Suggestion schemes can work provided that people on all sides know that:

- All ideas from everyone will be listened to.
- Every idea deserves thanks.
- Some ideas will not work.
- A forum for ideas assists in the process of innovation.

Recognition (and selection) of the ideas to be pursued should be on the basis that the idea can show:

- Originality of thought.
- An ultimate benefit to the customer.
- Business potential.
- Quality improvement.
- Cost savings.
- Viability in implementation.

When sieving ideas, you should ask three questions (as Henry Ford did):

1 Is it needed?
2 Is it practical?
3 Is it commercial?

'If in doubt, try it out.'

Idea 68: Using brainstorming to generate ideas

Brainstorming is one way of getting a large number of ideas from a group in a short time. The ideas that are produced then have to be sieved and tested.

These simple, well-tried rules for brainstorming are hard to beat:

- *Suspend judgment* – no criticism or evaluation.
- *Free-wheel* – anything goes, the wilder the better.
- *Quantity* – the more ideas the merrier.
- *Combine and improve* – link ideas, improve suggested ones.

When leading a brainstorming session the four main steps are:

1. *Introduce* – explain the aim of the session and remind people of Osborn's rules.
2. *Warm up* – if necessary do a practice exercise (e.g. 20 uses for a hammer).
3. *State the problem* – not too detailed.
4. *Guide* – to provide time to think and in the following:
    - Generation of ideas.
    - No judgment/criticism/evaluation!
    - Clarification.
    - Maintaining a free flow of ideas.

When leading a session that is 'sticky' and short of ideas to start with, ask 'what if?' questions to stimulate thought.

Brainstorming sessions should always be followed up, perhaps in smaller groups. Ideas should then be evaluated by:

- Deciding the selection criteria.
- Selecting obvious winning ideas.
- Eliminating unworkable ideas.
- Sifting ideas into groups and selecting the best in each.
- Applying the selection criteria to obvious winners and identify the 'best of' the various groups.
- Testing the selections by 'reverse brainstorming' (i.e. in how many ways can this idea fail?).
- Informing participants of further developments.

You can achieve successful brainstorming by managers by asking yourself these questions:

- Do you use It whenever appropriate?
- Does it work? If not, are you leading it effectively?
- Is there a better person than you to lead a session?
- Can you point to where brainstorming sessions have improved creative thinking in your organization?
- Do you and your managers have a list of problems that could benefit from brainstorming?
- Do you use teams sufficiently to work on problems?

Do I spend more time on 'brainstorming' than 'blamestorming'?

When taking good ideas to market, here are a number of questions you should apply to your organization.

Checklist for the generation of ideas

- ☐ Is there an internal market for innovative ideas?
- ☐ Do teams allocate time to consider ideas?
- ☐ Do you and your teams spend time away from the office to review performance and plans?
- ☐ Are customers/suppliers involved in innovation in your business?
- ☐ Do you have successfully innovative teams and/or individuals and can you identify reasons for their success?
- ☐ Do you have a suggestion scheme that works?
- ☐ Are new ideas properly rewarded?
- ☐ Do you help ensure that new ideas are not lost through poor presentation?
- ☐ Do you know of an alternative route to profitability and growth other than through innovation?

Follow-up test

Decision making

- ☐ Have you agreed the aims and objectives with the team?
- ☐ Have you involved the team in collecting and sifting the relevant information?
- ☐ Has the team helped you to generate a number of possible courses of action?
- ☐ Have you used the synergy of team members' minds to firm up the feasible options?
- ☐ Have you tested for consensus to see how far, in the circumstances, a course of action you favour is seen to be the optimum one?
- ☐ Have you secured everyone's commitment to make it work?
- ☐ Have you reviewed the decision with the team so that the lessons of success and failure are learnt for the future?

Creativity and innovation

- ☐ Would you describe yourself as good at visualizing things you haven't directly experienced?
- ☐ Has anyone praised you for your imagination within the last year?
- ☐ Have you invented or made anything recently, at work or in your leisure time, that definitely required imagination?

- ☐ Do you tend to foresee accurately what happens before the event?
- ☐ Where possible, do you build into your plans time to 'sleep on it', so as to give your depth mind an opportunity to contribute?
- ☐ Do you deliberately seek to employ your depth mind to help you to:
  - ◆ Analyze a complex situation?
  - ◆ Restructure a problem?
  - ◆ Reach value judgments?
- ☐ Have you experienced waking up next morning to find that your unconscious mind has resolved some problem or made some decision for you?
- ☐ Do you see your depth mind as being like a computer? Remember the computer proverb: Garbage in, garbage out.
- ☐ Do you keep a notebook or pocket recorder at hand to capture fleeting or half-formed ideas?
- ☐ Do you think you can benefit from understanding how other people's depth minds work?
- ☐ Is your team noted for its creative ideas and willingness to try new ways or methods?
- ☐ Can you now clearly see the barriers to innovation in organizations and how they can be overcome by good leadership?

PART FIVE

The Challenge of Strategic Leadership

Leadership exists at three broad levels: team, operational and leadership. In Part Five we shall explore together the generic role of the strategic leader and its seven constituent functions.

There is an underlying unity in strategic leadership, whatever field you are in and however structured or unstructured your work in it may be. Walter Bagehot, a nineteenth-century banker, economist and journalist famous for his insights into economics and political questions, understood this well:

> *The summits of the various kinds of business are, like the tops of mountains, much more alike than the parts below – the bare principles are much the same; it is only the rich variegated details of the lower strata that so contrast with one another.*

> *But it needs travelling to know that the summits are the same. Those who live on one mountain believe that their mountain is wholly unlike all others.*

Don't think of these levels of leadership exclusively in terms of large organizations. Leaders at all levels need to think in terms of these team, operational and strategic functions, and this is especially true for leaders of small or medium-sized businesses.

Five Greatest Ideas for the Role of Strategic Leader

Idea 69: Levels of leadership

Leadership exists on different levels. Thinking of organizations, there are three broad levels or domains of leadership, as shown in the diagram and the table.

The need is for excellence at all three levels of leadership. The secret to business success lies in teamwork between and within each of these levels.

Levels of leadership

Levels of leadership	
Strategic	The leader of a whole organization, with a number of operational leaders under their personal direction.
Operational	The leader of one of the main parts of the organization, with more than one team leader under their control. It is already a case of being a leader of leaders.
Team	The leader of a team of some 10 to 20 people with clearly specified tasks to achieve.

A simple recipe for organizational success is to have effective leaders occupying these roles and working together in harmony as a team.

Idea 70: The art of being a leader-in-chief

> *There are many paths to the top of the mountain, but the view is always the same.*
>
> Chinese proverb

Strategy (*strategia* in Greek) originally meant strategic leadership – the art of being a commander-in-chief.

Strategy is in fact made up of two ancient Greek words. The first part comes from *stratos*, which means an army spread out as in camp, and thus a large body of people. The second part, *-egy*, comes from the Greek verb 'to lead'. There is a rough breathing mark in the Greek giving an *h* sound, which explains the spelling of the English word *hegemony* – meaning the leadership of one nation over others – which is derived from it.

It was Athens, rivaled only by Sparta, which claimed the hegemony of the Greek city states. Around 500BC a senior commander in the Athenian army came to be called a *strategos*, a leader of the army. The English word we use to translate this word is *general*. It literally means something (or someone) that is applicable to the whole. So a military general is the person who is accountable for the whole army as well as its parts.

Therefore the role of a strategic leader is to do for the whole what other leaders should accomplish for the parts.

Strategia, the art of being a commander-in-chief, includes not just formulating strategy (in our modern sense) but also good administration, good communications, and the training and equipping of the soldiers under one's command. It is a *leadership* word.

Most of the functions and qualities of strategic leadership are transferable from one field to another. The early Greeks gave us some examples: selecting, punishing and rewarding, building alliances, and being hard-working.

Some qualifications of a strategic leader are natural and some are acquired. Chief among them is the ability to win the goodwill of those under you.

Idea 71: Seven functions of strategic leadership

If you wish to know a man, give him authority.

Bulgarian proverb

Leadership can be compared to light. Light can be refracted – as Newton demonstrated – into three primary colours: red, green and blue. If you put these three colours into the three circles model (in place of task, team and individual), the intersection triangle in the middle is light.

Using a prism, Newton was then able to refract light into the seven conventional colours of the rainbow: red, orange, yellow, green, blue, indigo and violet. You can think of these colours as representing the seven main functions into which the generic role of leader breaks down.

Working from some first principles of organizations, the generic role of strategic leadership (or *strategia*) refracts into seven colours or functions, which are, in no order of importance:

- Giving direction for the organization as a whole.
- Strategic thinking and strategic planning.
- Making it happen.
- Relating the parts to the whole.
- Building key partnerships and other social relationships.
- Releasing the corporate spirit.
- Choosing and developing leaders for today and tomorrow.

Idea 72: Seven useful skills for operational leaders

Behind an able man there are always other able men.

Chinese proverb

A common factor for all operational leaders is that they should have direct engagement with the strategic agenda of the organization, however small the requirement for that engagement may be.

In order at their level to meet their responsibilities for task, team and individual areas, operational leaders need some special skills.

My colleague Dr. David Faraday has listed seven of these skills:

- *Influencing* – influencing upwards, both to more senior operational levels and to the strategic level; influencing peers; and recognizing, assessing and accepting the influence of others.
- *Informing* – gathering and communicating information from above, from below and across different parts of the organization.
- *Interpreting* – understanding and translating strategic and higher-level operational decisions, or requirements, into language and activities that will be used at lower levels within the organization.
- *Initiating* – creating, developing and putting into practice new initiatives, and supporting this practice at lower levels within the organization.
- *Implementing* – putting the strategic plan into operation and supporting this implementation appropriately at all levels.
- *Networking* – creating and building relationships with others, both within and outside the organization.

- *Succession planning* – ensuring ongoing leadership provision within the organization.

These functions reflect the essential core of what an operational leader has to do. As might be expected, these functions predominantly relate to communication flow and making things happen. This has to be achieved within the bounds of the organization's requirements, or constraints, as identified at the strategic level.

Finally, it is important to emphasize that these operational functions need to be carried out in addition to the functions required of a team leader.

As an operational leader, your skills in two-way communication upward, downward and sideways – and building trust in all three directions – are vital. You are the link between strategy and action.

Idea 73: Practical wisdom

> *Reason and calm judgement, the qualities especially belonging to a leader.*
>
> Tacitus

An effective strategic leader needs, above all else, practical wisdom. This phrase best translates the Greek word *phronesis*, which the Roman rendered as *prudentia* – hence our English word prudence. Practical wisdom is a blend of *intelligence*, *experience* and *goodness*.

Experience – of both the world and of the particular field or business – and moral goodness are self-explanatory. The kind of eager, alert, outreaching mental quality that marks out the leader predisposes them to use their powers in versatile ways:

- To see the point.
- To sense relationships and analogies quickly.
- To identify the essentials in a complex picture.
- To 'put two and two together'.
- To find the salient factors in past experience that are helpful in shedding light on present difficulties.
- To be able to distinguish clearly between ends and means.
- To appraise situations readily.
- To see their significance in the total setting of present and past experience.
- To get the cue as to the likely line of wise action.

These overlap considerably, but taken together they offer an idea of the kind of practical intelligence or sense we are talking about.

Remember that your position does not give you the right to command. It only lays upon you the duty of so living your life that others may receive your orders without being humiliated.

Dag Hammarskjöld, writing as Secretary-General of the United Nations

Seven Greatest Ideas for Strategic Leadership Skills

Idea 74: Giving direction

Without a vision the people perish.

Book of Proverbs

The art of strategic leadership is to locate the right direction and to steer the ship that way and not another. It is simple but not easy.

There should be three sources for generating a sense of direction.

Purpose

The overarching, general or integrating task of the group or organization.

Your defined purpose answers the *why* questions – 'Why are we in business?' 'Why are we doing this?' It can signify too the content of value or meaning in what you are doing.

Human nature craves meaning, and so if your purpose connects with personal and moral values, you will not find it difficult to generate a *sense of purpose* in your team – and here *purpose* means *energy*. Your team organization will be under way, like a ship at sea.

Values

'We had our personal differences,' said Winston Churchill, talking about President de Gaulle, 'but we navigated by the same stars.'

Values are the stars you navigate by in life. You will never reach a star – it is not a destination like the port of Rotterdam. But a single star or a constellation can give you direction.

In the plural, values signify the principles or moral standards of a person, group or organization: what is considered to be valuable and

important. The assumption is that these are basic beliefs and convictions that govern behaviour.

Vision

Purpose is not the same as *vision*. A vision is a mental picture of what you want the team or the organization to look like or be in, say, three years' time.

Where an organization or a team, a nation or a community has a common vision of its future being – the desired state or condition it holds up before itself even in the dark days – it will also have as a by-product a sense of direction. It will know the difference between moving in one direction rather than another, between progress and regress.

Where there is a vision in this sense you do not have to drive people forwards: the music of the vision *draws* them in a certain direction.

1. Am I clear about the purpose of my organization, what it is meant to do and be?
2. Do all members of my organization understand *why* what they are doing is worthwhile?
3. Would I say that everyone has a *common* purpose, whatever their roles or responsibilities?
4. Can I identify and write down the three key values or moral principles that guide my organization?
5. Do I think that any changes are needed in these values? (If the answer is yes, write down the new set of values.)
6. Have I developed a widely shared vision of what sort of organization I am building for the future?
7. If so, could I produce for my colleagues a kind of sketch map in words of what it would look like?

Idea 75: Strategic thinking and strategic planning

All men can see the tactics whereby I conquer, but what none can see is the strategy out of which great victory is evolved.

Sun Tzu (fourth century BC)

Strategic thinking is thinking about the longer term – the more important ends in any situation, and the pathways that may or may not lead to them.

There are three characteristics of strategic thinking: it considers what is important, the longer term and multiple factors.

Importance

The starting point is the ability to distinguish between the important, the less important and the unimportant. If something is important it is marked by or possesses weight or consequence. The urgent is not always important; the important is not always urgent.

Longer term

How long is long? That all depends. But *strategic* implies a longer-term perspective rather than a short-term view. Indeed, to think strategically may mean trading short-term gain for long-term advantage.

Multi-factor

Take all the factors or elements relevant to the overall end into account, not just one – however important that may be.

Strategic planning

Strategic thinking has to issue a strategic *plan* that clears the desk for action; otherwise it degenerates into strategic daydreaming. The process of strategic planning is a two-way and highly interactive one between you as the strategic leader and the operational leaders who head up the 'strategic business units' (as they were first called by General Electric) or their equivalents.

What is critical is the 'one-liners' from the top – simple directives to particular parts of the organization or, in a federal set-up, to organizations within the group – that point each 'part' to an achievable mission that is coherent with, and contributing toward, the overall strategy.

1 Does my organization have a strategy that fits its purpose, values and vision?
2 Do I revise and re-evaluate that strategy in the light of changing circumstances?
3 Have I developed a strategy that is as simple as possible, rather than complicated?
4 Is the strategic plan flexible enough for modern conditions?
5 Have I listened to the strategic ideas, questions and creative thinking from my advisers and senior colleagues?
6 Does my strategic plan include 'success criteria' for measuring its overall results?

Idea 76: Making it happen

Between the idea
And the reality
Between the motion
And the act
Falls the Shadow

T S Eliot (1888–1965), *The Hollow Men* (1925)

These days many strategic leaders, in both private and public sectors of organizational life, are called chief executive – a shortened form of the American title chief executive officer (CEO). To execute means to put into effect, to perform, to carry out what exists in plan or intent – in short, to *make it happen*.

'A log of wood may lie in the river for years but it never becomes a crocodile,' says a trenchant African proverb. Many managers are promoted to the role of strategic leader but lack leadership ability: they are logs, not crocodiles. This functional area of strategic leadership is one of real weakness for them. They can – with help from others – agree purpose, values and vision; they can even draw up impressive and detailed strategic plans; but *it does not happen*. The vision remains a dream; the strategic plan remains merely a piece of paper. Eventually people come to realize that what they hear from their chief executive is the sound of a hollow log, but by then it is too late. Like the dawn, opportunity waits for no organization.

> *No one would have doubted his ability to reign, had he never been emperor.*
>
> Roman historian Tacitus (AD 56–117),
> writing about Emperor Galba

Contrast such a useless chief executive with an effective strategic leader. They know that a key part of their role is to oversee the

implementation of the strategic plan. It is not their job to conduct the actual business of achieving the common task – that is the responsibility of operational and team leaders.

A wise general will visit his field commanders, overseeing the implementation of the agreed strategic plan. But you should remember to leave tactics to your operational and team leaders – don't interfere unnecessarily, especially if things are going broadly to plan.

'How is it that you spend so much time out of your office?' I once asked the President of Toyota. 'In my home country,' I explained, 'chief executives tend to be more or less invisible, like badgers. They inhabit the executive suite of corporate headquarters, sitting behind their desks dealing with paperwork all day or attending meetings. It is as if their business is meetings. They tell me that they haven't got time to get out of head office. Why do you do it so differently?'

'The reason is really very simple,' the President replied with a smile. '*We do not make Toyota cars in my office*!'

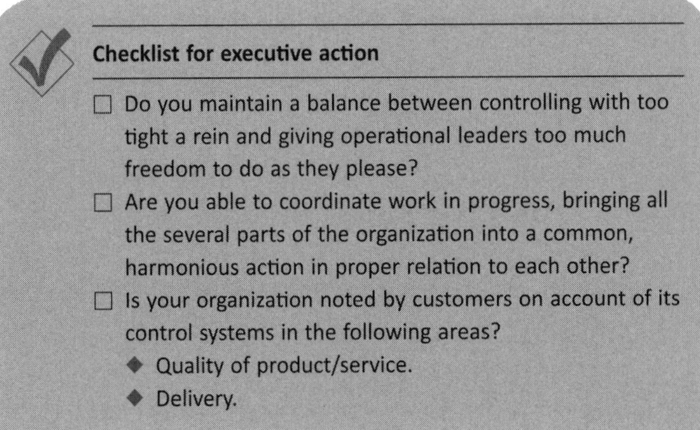

Checklist for executive action

- ☐ Do you maintain a balance between controlling with too tight a rein and giving operational leaders too much freedom to do as they please?
- ☐ Are you able to coordinate work in progress, bringing all the several parts of the organization into a common, harmonious action in proper relation to each other?
- ☐ Is your organization noted by customers on account of its control systems in the following areas?
  - ◆ Quality of product/service.
  - ◆ Delivery.

- Keeping costs down.
- Safety.

☐ Does your strategic plan have provision for regular progress reviews?

☐ Do you visit all parts of the organization on a regular basis?

☐ Do you always take action if a leader in your organization fails to do what they committed themselves to do?

☐ Do all the individual leaders in the organization work together as a high-performance leadership team?

Idea 77: Relating the parts to the whole

Dux erat ille ducum (He was a leader of leaders)

Ovid (43 BC–17/18 AD), *Heroides*

One major issue in all organizations is getting the right balance between the whole and the parts. Therefore, the fourth generic function of a strategic leader is to *create harmony*: to bring together the 'discordant elements' into 'one society'.

Alfred P Sloan who, along with Albert du Pont, had an immense influence on corporate organization in the United States, saw that as the key issue for working out his relations with the management team. Writing in *My Years with General Motors* (1964), he expressed it thus:

> *Good management rests on a reconciliation of centralization and decentralization, or 'decentralization with coordinated control'.*

For 'centralization' here read *whole*, and for 'decentralization' read *part*. Sloan's solution, as he hinted in his last phrase, is *both–and*: decentralize as much as you can but maintain some essential control from the centre.

That sounds simple, but in practice it is not easy to achieve. No formula exists, whatever the popular pundits or gurus on 'organizational behaviour' may say. As a strategic leader you may have to be able to think it out for yourself and make some flexible adjustments as life changes. As Sloan continued:

> *There is no hard and fast rule for sorting out the various responsibilities and the best way to assign them. The balance which is struck… varies according to what is being decided, the circumstances of the time, past experience, and the temperaments and skills of the executive involved.*

Idea 78: Building partnerships

When spiders' webs unite, they can tie up a lion

Ethiopian proverb

Among the transferable skills of a strategic leader that Socrates identified is attracting allies and helpers. Here I shall call it *building partnerships* – the fifth generic function of strategic leadership.

The principal necessary condition for a successful alliance or partnership, then, is a shared common aim. The attainment of the end in view, of course, needs to be strongly in the interests of both parties, however they define their interests. If the potential contributions of the partners to the common end are complementary, like those of team members in a real team, so much the better.

Whenever you enter into a partnership or work in a mixed team of 'insiders' and 'outsiders', use the three circles model to clarify:

- What is our common *task*?
- How can we best work together as a *team*?
- How can each *individual* (part or organization) give their best?

Always take seriously the interests of your partner or ally. Make sure that they are getting *their* share of benefit from the mutual enterprise. Make it a win–win story.

Checklist for building partnerships

- ☐ Do you now see building partnerships as one of the key functions in your role as strategic leader?
- ☐ Do you balance the time you spend in the organization and the time you spend outside the organization building strategic relations with key players – such as allies, customers, suppliers?
- ☐ Could your organization achieve more if you joined forces with other partners?
- ☐ If you consider your products and services, your employment policies and the effects your organization has on the environment, is your organization socially responsible?
- ☐ Does your organization confer benefits other than employment on its local communities?
- ☐ Does your organization work well with colleagues from other organizations, nations or cultures?

Can I transcend nationality and gender and work as a person with other people in international teams to accomplish global goals?

Idea 79: Releasing the corporate spirit

The task of leadership is not to put greatness into humanity, but to elicit it, for the greatness is there already.

John Buchan (1875–1940), British novelist and politician

Remember that purpose can also be regarded as a form of energy, somewhat like gravity, as well as being another word for your long-term or ultimate aim. Aims arise, we could say, when purpose is directed and harnessed. Purpose here is energy plus direction – engineers call it a vector. It is comparable to being under way.

You will be familiar now with the idea that leadership is about showing the way: the path or road ahead. In the nautical context, way also implies the power that is moving a ship forward. So we talk about a ship as being 'under way'. To lose way, on the other hand, is to lose momentum when sailing; to 'gather way' is to pick up speed again. We talk of a project as being 'now well under way'.

As the Scottish proverb says, 'The clan is greater than the chief.' A critical factor about teams or organizations is what the French call their *esprit de corps*, group feeling or power. The leader who can command it to best effect will be stronger.

As a strategic leader, then, your task – as John Buchan says at the head of this chapter – is not to put greatness into people, as if you were filling up a car with petrol. See it differently: the greatness is there already. You are there to elicit it, not for your own ends or interests, but in pursuit of a common purpose that has real value. That should be your vision of people as a leader; that is how you should see your organization.

Great generals of the past – military strategic leaders – have shown the way for today's strategic leaders. They created a sense of partnership with their soldiers by the habit of talking to them. Apart from

sharing the dangers and hardships of their soldiers, they therefore also shared with them the aim and the strategy for achieving it, thus taking the soldiers into their confidence.

'Out of this habit', Eisenhower said, 'grows mutual confidence, a feeling of partnership that is the essence of *esprit de corps*'. It always works – why not try it yourself?

> *I made the soldiers partners with me in the battle. I always told them what I was going to do and what I wanted them to do. I think the soldiers felt that they mattered, that they belonged.*
>
> Field Marshall Montgomery (1887–1976)

1 'The human spirit has a greatness in it that enables people on occasion to do extraordinary things.' Do I agree with this statement?
2 Have I ever known a leader who seemed to be able to release the greatness in people?
3 Which of these statements applies more to me:
   - I do not trust people until they have proved themselves to be trustworthy.
   - I trust people until such a time as they show themselves to be untrustworthy.
4 Do I now have a clear idea of what my organization expects of its strategic, operational and team leaders?

Idea 80: Developing today's and tomorrow's leaders

You are not born a leader, you become one.

Proverb of the Balimbe tribe in West Africa

The seventh function of strategic leadership is to select and train leaders at strategic, operational and team leadership levels. Again, as a strategic leader you should take ownership of that challenge – and it will be no surprise to you that here as elsewhere you should lead from the front.

The position is that we do know how to train team leaders, based on the three circles model of the generic role of leader, though largely through ignorance that hard-won know-how is grossly underused. That is the foundation.

Practice and reflection are the ways in which those individuals with an aptitude for leadership at operational and strategic levels prepared themselves – or are prepared – for these roles.

Some chief executives make the mistake of regarding only themselves and their fellow directors as leaders and the rest as managers. Diligent readers of this book will not fall into that common fallacy. Indeed, looking even beyond the all-important team leaders, it is possible to see all of your employees as leaders in their own way. That makes you into a 'leader of leaders'.

Few organizations are really geared toward developing to the full the *leadership potential* within them. Sometimes this may be due to the fact that they place little or no premium on it, assuming either that it is not important or that the conventional management training will provide it. Only the best organizations show a real and sustained commitment to selecting and developing their business

leaders. Why? Because those organizations know from experience that effective leadership at all levels is essential for their continued success.

Seize opportunities for talking to your managers about leadership, not in an academic sense but about what it means to you personally and why you think it is important. On a one-to-one basis with your operational leaders, do not hesitate to offer them advice drawn from your own practical wisdom.

In both success and failure, there are leadership lessons to be harvested.

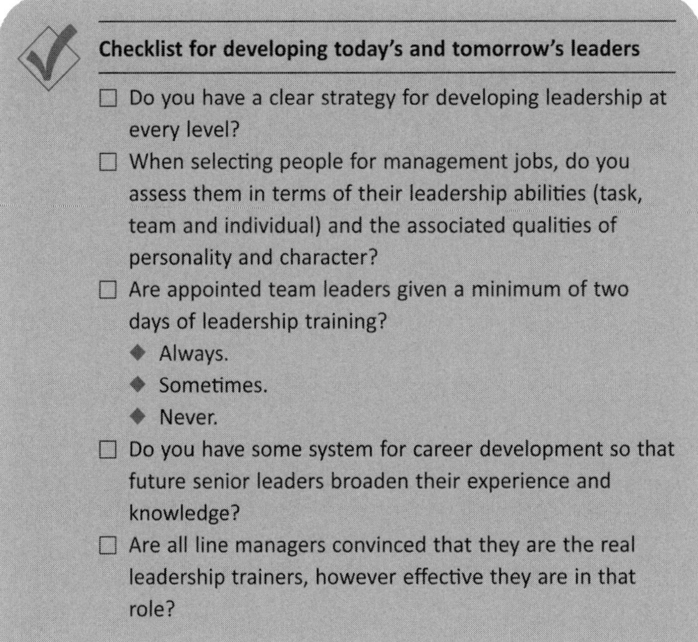

Checklist for developing today's and tomorrow's leaders

- ☐ Do you have a clear strategy for developing leadership at every level?
- ☐ When selecting people for management jobs, do you assess them in terms of their leadership abilities (task, team and individual) and the associated qualities of personality and character?
- ☐ Are appointed team leaders given a minimum of two days of leadership training?
  - Always.
  - Sometimes.
  - Never.
- ☐ Do you have some system for career development so that future senior leaders broaden their experience and knowledge?
- ☐ Are all line managers convinced that they are the real leadership trainers, however effective they are in that role?

- ☐ Is there a specialist 'research and development' team that is keeping the organization and its line managers up to date – and up to the mark?
- ☐ Has your organizational structure been evolved with good leadership in mind?
- ☐ Do leaders, actual or potential, realize that they are the ones who 'own' their self-development?
- ☐ Would you say that there was room for improving the organizational culture or ethos?
  - A great deal.
  - Some.
  - None.
- ☐ Are your top leaders really behind leadership development?
  - Wholeheartedly.
  - Half-heartedly.
  - Not yet.

Follow-up test

The role of the strategic leader

- ☐ Do you now have a clear idea of the role and responsibilities of a strategic leader?
- ☐ Are you aware that the art of *strategia* – being a leader-in-chief – requires much more of you than defining corporate strategy in the narrow sense?
- ☐ Have you grasped the essential functions required to be an effective leader at three levels (team, operational and strategic)?

Strategic leadership skills

- ☐ Has your organization a clear sense of direction, stemming from a common purpose, a positive set of values and a realistic vision for the future?
- ☐ Does your high-quality strategic thinking lead to strategic planning that both involves and commits the key players?
- ☐ Do you and your top team ensure that it happens?
- ☐ 'The parts work together in the whole harmoniously and with the minimum of friction.' How far does that description fit your organization?
- ☐ Have you achieved the optimum balance – in present circumstances – between centralization and decentralization?

- ☐ How much of your time do you spend on building good relations with your key partners and allies?
- ☐ Are you an ambassador for your organization in the local community and society at large – not least its elected representative government?
- ☐ List three ways in which you go about releasing the corporate spirit – energy, creativity and generosity:

  i

  ii

  iii
- ☐ Do you take direct personal responsibility for senior leadership appointments and ensure that the organization has a strategy for developing its leaders?

PART SIX

Developing Your Personal Skills

Great leaders are all effective communicators both one on one and in larger groups, using the written or spoken word as appropriate. Unless you can get your message across and take on board what others are trying to tell you, then you simply will not be effective as a leader in any kind of business.

To be a good communicator, you need to develop your personal communication skills, your ability to lead communications groups and your effectiveness in the downward, upward and sideways flows of information and ideas in organizations.

You need to develop your understanding of the nature of communication and the key skills of speaking and listening, particularly as they can be used in interviews, meetings and communicating within organizations.

Another set of key personal skills that all effective leaders require relates to time management. If you can't manage your time you can't manage anything! Time to think, time for people, time for significant allies, partners and customers – these are the rewards of being an effective time manager.

It is essential for you as a strategic leader to make time to think, both about the present and the future. That means in the first place having an awareness of the value of time and the economical use of it.

'Ask me for anything,' Napoleon used to say, 'except for time.' He knew that he had only 24 hours a day like anyone else, but he used his time most effectively. Do you?

Twelve Greatest Ideas for Effective Communication

Idea 81: 15 key issues in communication

It is self-evident that written and spoken communication skills are of crucial importance in business (and personal) life. Managers and leaders must be effective communicators, good at getting their message across and at drawing the best out of people. Communication skills in all forms, including non-verbal communication, need to be worked at and improved to ensure that you understand people and they understand you.

The 15 key issues to be aware of in communication are:

1 You must be in social contact with the other person or people.
2 You must want to communicate.
3 It is better to risk familiarity than be condemned for remoteness.
4 The best way to empower others is to impart information (along with the delegated authority to make decisions and act on the information given).
5 Get out of your office – meet, listen, provide information and give people the context in which to operate – to communicate and encourage.
6 Good communication is the core of customer care.
7 Remember that customers (and suppliers) communicate with others about you.
8 To communicate with your customers you must handle complaints (as an organization) as personally as possible – by a meeting or phone call in preference to a letter or email. You must listen to what customers suggest and communicate product/service changes or developments to them in advance.
9 Presentation skills are important in communicating with colleagues as well as customers/clients.

10 Meetings, internal and external, are key indicators of a person's communication skills, including listening.
11 Communication is a business requirement: establish proper systems and ensure that everyone uses them.
12 Remember the equation size + geographical distance = communication problems.
13 Communicate with poor performers to improve their contribution and in appraisals be truthful, helpful and tactful.
14 Help others to improve their communication skills.
15 Assess your own communication skills and strive to improve them bit by bit. (Also, assess the communication skills of colleagues and identify areas for improvement.)

'Don't assume that communication is actually happening – double-check.'

1 Do I understand the importance of communication in my personal and business life?
2 Am I a good communicator? (Check with your partner at home, with friends and with colleagues.)
3 Can I write down my strengths and weaknesses as a communicator? Make sure you list them.
4 Have I identified a need to improve my communication skills in any or all of these areas within my organization, and will I now set about doing so (reading further books and/or attending training seminars as needs be):
   - Listening?
   - One-to-one communication?
   - Speaking and presentation?
   - Managing meetings?
5 Am I strongly motivated to become an excellent communicator?

Idea 82: Listening – a key element in communication

Listening has been called the forgotten skill in communication. It is more than just hearing, it is giving thoughtful attention to another person while they are speaking and being open to what they say.

The 'disease of not listening', as Shakespeare called it, has the following symptoms:

- Selective listening – turning a deaf ear to certain types of information that you don't want to hear. If you are a selective listener, people edit what they tell you and that can be damaging, both in business and in private life.
- Continual and badly timed interrupting.
- Day-dreaming – letting your mind wander.
- Easily being distracted by external factors, such as noise or temperature.
- Refusing to listen to anything that appears to be difficult to understand.
- Over-reacting to a speaker's delivery and/or the quality of their visual aids rather than concentrating on what is being said.

The tell-tale signs of a good listener are:

- Paying close attention to others when they are talking.
- Taking an interest in someone you meet for the first time, trying to find an area of mutual interest.
- Believing that everyone has something of value to teach or impart to you.
- Setting aside a person's personality or voice in order to concentrate on what they know.

- Being curious in people, ideas and things.
- Encouraging the speaker (with nods or eye contact).
- Taking notes.
- Knowing one's own prejudices and working at controlling them to ensure that listening continues.
- Being patient with poor communicators.
- Not being told that you don't listen.
- Having an open mind in respect of other people's points of view.

People have two eyes and two ears and only one tongue – which suggests that they ought to look and also listen twice as much as they speak.

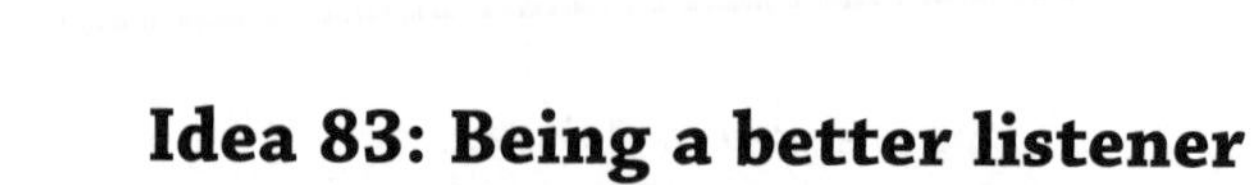

Idea 83: Being a better listener – developing listening skills

Listening skills centre on the following five attributes:

1. Being willing to listen.
2. Clearly hearing the message.
3. Interpreting the meaning (the speaker's meaning, not only your interpretation).
4. Evaluating carefully (suspending judgment at first but then assessing value and usefulness).
5. Responding appropriately – remembering that communication is a two-way street.

In active listening you must be prepared to:

- Ask questions.
- Weigh the evidence.
- Watch your assumptions.
- Listen between the lines (at what is not said and for non-verbal elements such as facial expressions, tone, posture, physical gestures etc.).

Idea 84: Six principles of effective speaking

Speaking takes many different forms, ranging from the formal – addresses, discourses, orations, lectures, homilies, sermons, presentations – to the less formal. Briefing your team usually falls into the second category.

These six principles apply to all the public speaking situations you will encounter as a leader. You don't have to be a great orator. Apply these principles and you will become an effective speaker:

1 *Be clear* – make your communication unclouded or transparent. A clear sky is one free of clouds, mists and haze. With reference to speech it means freedom from any confusion and hence easy to understand. Being clear is not primarily a matter of sentences and words. The value of clarity is an inner one: it should act as a principle, purifying thought at its source, in the mind.

2 *Be prepared* – take active, conscious deliberation and effort before action. To be unprepared, by contrast, means that you have not thought or made any attempt at readying yourself for what you know you may or will have to face. You are like a football team that never trains or plans before its matches.

3 *Be simple* – so that your hearers are not put off by the unnecessarily complicated or intricate. But don't oversimplify or talk down to your audience, even if they are children.

4 *Be vivid* – make it come alive! This graphic or colourful quality springs from the interest and enthusiasm in the mind and heart of the communicator, but it has to become visible in your language.

5 *Be natural* – or, if you prefer, be yourself. What you say and how you say it should reflect your own personality.

6 *Be concise* – be economical with your words and other people's time. Less is more.

Idea 85: Profiling the occasion – the first element of a good presentation

When planning a presentation, there is one thing you should do before anything else: profile the occasion, the audience and the location.

You should ask yourself the following questions.

The occasion

- What kind is it?
- What are its aims?
- What time is allotted?
- What else is happening?

The audience

- Do they know anything about you?
- Do you know its size?
- What do they expect?
- Why are they there?
- What is their knowledge level?
- Do you know any of them personally/professionally?
- Do you expect friendliness, indifference or hostility?
- Will they be able to use what they hear?

The location

- Do you know the room size, seating arrangements, lay-out/set-up and acoustics?
- Do you know the technical arrangements for the use of microphones, audio-visuals, lighting, and whether

assistance is available (and have you notified in advance your requirements)?

- Do you know who will control room temperature, lighting and moving people in and out?
- Have you seen it/should you see it?

Remember the soldier's proverb: Time spent on reconnaissance is seldom wasted.

When making a presentation, do I always check the occasion, the audience and the location?

Idea 86: Planning and writing the presentation

The key elements in planning and writing your presentation are:

1 Deciding your objective, which needs to be:
   - Clear.
   - Specific.
   - Measurable.
   - Achievable in the time available.
   - Realistic.
   - Challenging.
   - Worthwhile.
   - Participative.
2 Making a plan with a framework which has:
   - A *beginning* (including introductory remarks, statement of objectives and relevance and an outline of the presentation).
   - A *middle* (divided into up to six sections maximum, ensuring that the main points are illustrated and supported by examples or evidence, use summaries and consider the time allocation carefully – and test it).
   - An *end* (summarize, linking conclusions with objectives and end on a high note).

     At all costs avoid the sequence of *beginning*, *muddle* and *no end*!
3 As up to 50 percent of information is taken in through the eyes, careful consideration should be given to the clear, simple and vivid use of audio-visuals. As the Chinese proverb says, 'A picture is worth a thousand words.'
4 Plan to give as much of your talk as you can without using notes – that takes some practice, but it is a skill

that leaders need and that you can acquire easily if you know what you are talking about.

Light a flame at the start of your presentation and keep it burning throughout.

Idea 87: How best to deliver your presentation on the day

Overall you should ensure that your presentation has the following characteristics:

- The *beginning* introduces you properly, captures the audience and gives the background, objectives and outline of your talk.
- The *middle* is kept moving along (indicating whether questions are to be asked as you go or at the end), with eye contact over the whole audience, at a reasonable pace, with varying voice and obvious enjoyment on your part.
- The *end* is signalled clearly and then goes off with a memorized flourish.
- *Questions* are audible to all (or repeated if not), answered with conciseness, stimulated by you asking some questions, dealt with courteously and with the lights on.
- The *conclusion* is a strong summary of the talk, there are questions or discussions and the presentation closes with words of thanks.

If you find that you are nervous – and experiencing fear and its physical manifestations is normal – remember to:

- Breathe deeply.
- Manage your hands.
- Look at your audience.
- Move well.
- Talk slowly.
- Compose and relax yourself.
- Remember that the audience is invariably on your side.

- Project forward to the end of the presentation and picture the audience applauding at the end.

Be clear, be simple, be vivid, be concise and be natural.

Idea 88: One-to-one interviews

One-to-one meetings have common characteristics in that they are (usually) pre-arranged, require preparation and have a definite purpose.

Unless it happens to be a dismissal, one-to-one interviews require the following:

- Both parties know the purpose of the meeting (notified in advance).
- The information to be exchanged should be considered in advance and answers at the meeting should be honest.
- As the interviewer you should keep control: stick to the point at issue and the time allocated and give the other party adequate time to talk (prompting by questions if necessary).

The structure of the interview should be as follows:

- The opening – setting the scene, the purpose and a relaxed atmosphere.
- The middle – stay with the purpose, listen, cover the agenda.
- The close – summarize, agree action, end naturally, not abruptly, on a positive note.

Sometimes it is useful to ask appropriate questions to obtain the required information or exchange. Questions to use are open-ended, prompting, probing, or what-if questions, while the ones to avoid (unless they are being used for specific reasons) are yes/no, closed, leading or loaded questions.

Do I know the purpose of this interview? Does the other person?

Idea 89: Appraising performance

Remember that your aim in an appraisal is to improve performance. Therefore you have to be skilled at communicating your perceptions of both the strengths and the weaknesses of the individual concerned. You must have data or information at hand to back up any observation you give. Above all, you must put your suggestions across so that they are acceptable and actionable by the individual. The best way to do that is to ask the individual to appraise his or her own performance against the organization's standing or continuing aims and specific objectives. Then agree with him or her an action plan for the future.

Thus, the function of appraising an individual's performance is only useful if it is the prelude to some form of learning or training. Even if the result of the interview is that you dismiss that person, or transfer him or her to another group, it can still be presented in a positive light as a lesson you have learnt together. As a leader you need to be in part a teacher or trainer of people. Conversely, a teacher has to be something of a leader.

Is it possible to teach yourself specific techniques, such as asking questions of different kinds that may be useful in appraisal interviews? The following could be useful examples:

- *Opening* – 'Tell me about your sales programme'.
- *Probing* – 'Is that the first time you have failed to meet a target?'
- *Factual* – 'Where were you when it happened?'
- *Reflective* – 'You obviously feel very disappointed and upset at what was said to you.'
- *Leading* – 'I suppose you will improve that next year?'
- *Limited choice* – 'If you had to choose between general HR work and industrial relations, which would it be?'

What matters more, however, is taking seriously your responsibilities for *developing the individual* as his or her mentor throughout the year, not just for an hour or two in a formal or semi-formal interview. You should be able to offer him or her your practical wisdom.

When giving any form of criticism, ask yourself:

- Do I always criticize individuals in private?
- Is my tone constructive?
- Do I keep it simple and accurate?
- Do I omit comparisons with others?
- Do I stick to the facts and observable impressions, avoiding any reference to the other person's motives?
- Do I avoid long preambles and apologizing for what I am saying?

Idea 90: Seven ways to receive criticism

As a leader you don't only give constructive criticism, sometimes you have to receive it. When receiving constructive criticism you should:

- Remain quiet and listen.
- Not find fault with the criticizing person.
- Not try to manipulate the appraiser by an emotional response, such as despair.
- Not try to change the subject.
- Not caricature or belittle the complaint.
- Not ascribe an ulterior motive to the criticizer.
- Give the impression that you understand the point.

In the face of any kind of criticism, you should be open to it and not instinctively ignore, deny or deflect it. Whether or not you accept all or part of it is a secondary issue.

When criticized, do I always try to grasp the point in its fullness before accepting or rejecting it?

When a man says you are a horse laugh at him.
When two men assert that you are a horse, give it a thought.
And when three men say you are a horse, you had better go and buy a saddle for yourself.

Hungarian folk saying

Idea 91: Communication and the management of meetings

Meetings are much maligned, but are they usually approached and handled as they should be? In general terms, if it is to work, any meeting needs:

- Planning.
- Informality.
- Participation.
- Purpose.
- Leadership.

That is the case whether the meeting is in committee or conference format.

A meeting must have a purpose and this can be one (or all) of the following:

- To pool available information.
- To make decisions.
- To let off steam/tension.
- To change attitudes.
- To instruct or teach.

You should always be prepared before chairing any meeting:

- Know in advance what information, reports, agenda, layout, technical data or equipment is required.
- Be clear about the purpose of the meeting.
- Inform other participants of the purpose and share, in advance, relevant information or documents.
- Have a timetable and agenda (and notify others of these in advance).

- Identify the main topics and an objective for each.
- Make the necessary housekeeping arrangements.

Chairing a meeting means that you should guide and control it, having defined its purpose, gatekeeping the discussions as appropriate (opening the meeting to some, closing discussion when necessary), summarizing, interpreting and concluding it with agreed decisions, on time.

The chairman's role in leading and refereeing effective meetings is to ensure that the following elements are handled correctly:

- *Aim* – after starting on time, to outline the purpose clearly.
- *Plan* – to prepare the agenda (and allocate time).
- *Guide* – to ensure effective discussion.
- *Crystallize* – to establish conclusions.
- *Act* – to gain acceptance and commitment and then to end on time.

In my meetings, do I know the purpose, have an agenda, canvas opinions, agree conclusions and win acceptance of any action needed?

Remember that meetings are groups of people and that groups can develop their own group personality. It can help to understand the latter by thinking about your particular group's:

- Level of conformity.
- Professional, social and moral values.

- Attitude to change.
- Prejudice.
- Levels of power or influence.

It follows that the method of running the meeting and making it effective depends on understanding and overcoming problems posed by the group personality as well as your primary responsibility of meeting the group needs – task, team and individual.

Idea 92: Communication within your organization

> *"Treat information as 'shareware'."*

Organizations have varying degrees of permanence, hierarchy and formal communication. Informal communication supplements the formal communication.

The content of communication in organizations should be in relation to the following:

1. The *task*:
   - The purpose, aims and objectives.
   - Plans.
   - Progress and prospects.
2. The *team*:
   - Changes in structure and deployment.
   - Ways to improve teamwork.
   - Ethos and values.
3. The *individual*:
   - Pay and conditions.
   - Safety, health and welfare.
   - Education and training.

The direction of the flows of communication within an organization must be *downward*, *upward* and *sideways*.

When making decisions about what to communicate, bear in mind the *must-know* priorities and distinguish them from the lower *should-know* or *could-know* priorities (see the following diagram).

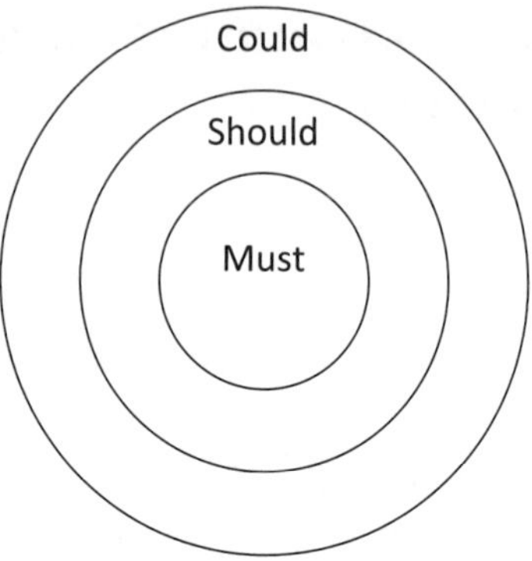

Priorities of 'need to know'

- MUST KNOW: vital points
- SHOULD KNOW: desirable but not essential
- COULD KNOW: relatively unimportant

The best way of communicating must-know items is face to face backed by the written word.

Two-way communication should be used and encouraged to:

- Communicate plans, changes, progress and prospects.
- Give employees the opportunity to change or improve management decisions (before they are made).
- Use the experience and ideas of employees to the full.
- Understand the other side's point of view.

Am I a good enough communicator?
What do others think? Do I even bother to find out, by communicating with them?

Eight Greatest Ideas for Managing Your Time

Idea 93: The ten principles of time management

Do I always make the best use of my time?
What can I do to save time and spend it wisely?

Time management is about managing your time with a focus on achievement: doing and completing those things that you want to do and that need doing.

Time management is goal driven and results oriented. Success in time management is measured by the quality of both your work and your personal life.

Tempus fugit

While it is true to say that life only makes sense in retrospect, it can be shaped by your sense of time and purpose. In keeping with business planning, *time* planning – and your approach to the use of your time (and to the extent that you can influence it, how others spend their time) – should avoid the trap of *failing to plan* – which is, in effect, planning to fail. In other words, if time is money, spend it wisely.

The basic approach to time management

You need to be certain that you:

- Can define your business leadership role and know what constitutes a successful outcome.
- Spend time thinking and planning for yourself and others.

- Have a clear understanding of your business purpose.
- Know the balance you wish to achieve between your business and your private commitments (and can identify the time demands on both).

Time management skills should be applied to your personal life as well as your business life.

The ten Adair principles of time management

Here are some practical suggestions to help you to make the best use of your time at work. Check yourself against this ten-point programme once a month for the next six months.

1 *Develop a personal sense of time.* Do not rely on memory or assume that you know where your time goes. For one or two weeks keep a record. Become more aware of the value of your time and resolve to use it well.

2 *Identify your longer-term goals and policies*. The clearer you are about your longer-term ends, the easier you will find it to identify your priorities. Policies are decisions about principles: they help you to make many daily decisions without having to waste too much time on them.

3 *Make middle-term plans*. You should be able fluently to translate *purpose* into *aims*, and *aims* into *objectives*. Plan your work on aims and objectives in terms of opportunities and desired results, priorities and deadlines.

4 *Plan the day*. Make a list of what you want to do each day. Arrange it or mark it according to some order of priority. Learn to say no, otherwise you will become merely a slave to the priorities of others.

5 *Make the best use of your best time*. Your best time is when you personally do your best work. Where possible, always use it for important tasks. Have some planned quiet periods for creative thinking.

6 *Organize your administrative work*. Work out systems for handling paperwork, dealing with emails and making telephone calls, so that you do not fragment your day. Make administration your servant and not your master.

7 *Manage meetings*. Work out the agenda carefully, allotting time for each item. Start on time and end on time. Use your skills as a leader to make meetings both businesslike and enjoyable. There is more on this in Idea 100.

8 *Delegate effectively*. Where possible, delegate as much administrative responsibility as you can. The reason for doing so is to free yourself for exercising the kind of leadership that your position requires. There is more on this in Idea 94.

9 *Make use of committed time*. Committed time is time given over to specific purposes, such as travel. Use waiting time or traveling time to think, plan, read or make calls. There is more on this in Idea 95.

10 *Manage your health*. Time management is primarily about the *quality* of your time, not about its *quantity.* Follow common-sense guidelines over sleep, diet, exercise and holidays. Achieve a balance between work and private life that works for you and keeps you free from the toxic kinds of stress. There is more on this in Idea 96.

Idea 94: Delegating effectively

Select the type of work for delegation and consider to whom it can best be delegated.

Type of work	Delegation to enact
1 Technical/specialist work	
a	a
b	b
c	c
2 Administrative/minor decisions	
a	a
b	b
c	c
3 Where others are more qualified	
a	a
b	b
c	c
4 Where staff development would result	
a	a
b	b
c	c

The seven main reasons why CEOs do not delegate were revealed by research in five European countries to be:

1. It is risky.
2. We enjoy doing things.
3. We dare not sit and think.
4. It is a slow process.
5. We like to be 'on top of everything'.
6. Will our subordinates outstrip us?
7. 'Nobody can do it as well as I can.'

So, what must you do to be a good delegator? There are five main tips:

1. Choose the right staff.
2. Train them.
3. Take care in briefing them, and ensuring their understanding of the 'why' and 'how to' of tasks delegated to them (and impart to them an understanding of business aims and policies).
4. Try not to interfere – stand back and support.
5. Control in a sensible and sensitive manner by checking progress at agreed intervals.

Checklist for effective delegation

- ☐ Do you take work home at evenings/weekends and/or work more than nine hours a day?
- ☐ Can you identify areas of work that you could/should delegate, but have not already done so?
- ☐ Do you define clearly the delegated tasks and satisfy yourself that the individual to whom they are delegated understands what is expected as an outcome?
- ☐ Can you trust people, or do you find it difficult to do so?
- ☐ Do you delegate authority and task?
- ☐ Do you think the delegated task will not be done as well by anyone else?
- ☐ Do you involve those to whom tasks have been delegated in the whole planning and problem-solving process?

'You will never have so much authority as when you begin to give it away.'

Idea 95: Making use of committed time

You can increase your level of achievement by using committed time (time that is 'booked', for example traveling or meal times) by, in the case of traveling time, ensuring that you use it to carry out reading, writing, thinking, having meetings, making phone calls; in the case of meal times, using them, where relevant, to hold business conversations or meetings.

In other words, you should establish productive activities to schedule alongside time that has to be committed to other activities:

- Daily routines: use dressing, bathtime/meals etc. to stimulate your mind.
- Waiting time: do not waste it – read or make phone calls.
- Travel time: use it productively – reading, planning or making phone calls.
- Television: do not let it consume too much of every evening – do something productive for yourself and your personal goals.

Idea 96: Managing your health and avoid stress

Time management has to be as much about ensuring that you maximize the amount of time you have available to use as about using time wisely. That means taking steps to ensure that you do not suffer time deprivation through illness of mind or body.

It is vital to look after your energy levels – to top up your batteries regularly – in order to fulfill your demanding role as a leader. Also, of course, you need to achieve and maintain a 'work–life balance' that works for you and your family, bearing in mind that nothing can change the fact that leadership – especially at the higher levels – *is* a very demanding job.

Research in 10 countries on 1000 managers reveals that improving time management can help eliminate the 12 most common sources of stress in managers, which are:

1. Time pressures and deadlines.
2. Work overload.
3. Inadequately trained subordinates.
4. Long working hours.
5. Attending meetings.
6. Demands of work on private and social life.
7. Keeping up with new technology.
8. Holding beliefs conflicting with those of the organization.
9. Taking work home.
10. Lack of power and influence.
11. The amount of travel required by work.
12. Doing a job below one's level of competence.

If you find yourself suffering from stress then you must:

- Do something about it: look at the stress factors and assess what can be done to change your life at work or at home.
- Express yourself: talk to people about how you are feeling and the concerns you have (even directly to a person who might be causing part of your stress).
- Evaluate priorities: check the balance of your life, take stock of activities and priorities and change them if necessary.
- Accept what you cannot control: have the courage to change the things that can be changed, the serenity to accept the things that cannot be changed and the wisdom to know the difference.
- Use your negative experience to change your behaviour positively.
- Use time management skills to take charge of your time and how it is spent, particularly making time to deal with stress-causing problems. Get them out of the way.
- Count your blessings – list those things that you are pleased with, about yourself or your achievements. Do not concentrate too much on the past (guilt) or the future (anxiety).
- Ask yourself: What is the worst that can happen and can I cope with that? Use this to reduce anxiety about an issue.

How many stress-related behaviours have I exhibited over the last 12 months?
What am I going to do about that – starting now?

Idea 97: Five techniques to keep interruptions brief

1. Meet people in their office whenever you can (you control your leaving time).
2. Stand rather than sit for casual visitors (this controls the length of their stay).
3. Keep a focus on time (mention the time you have available, refer to your next meeting and have a visible and watched clock).
4. Stick to the point and avoid butterflying from the main topic to unrelated ones.
5. Be firm in a pleasant way.

Idea 98: Six organizing ideas to improve time management

The killing of time is the worst of murders.

Daniel Defoe

1. Arrange your office or office space for ease of work, comfort and efficiency. Few people give this any thought at all.
2. Operate a clear desk policy – concentration is helped by doing one thing at a time, so your desk should only have on it the specific job that you are tackling at the time.
3. Write effectively, keeping it short and simple by thinking of the main point first and ordering your thoughts for logical expression.
4. Telephone – keep a log to see how time efficient you are now! Then get used to planning for each call you make (the salient points you want to make); grouping incoming and outgoing calls (usually for the end of the day when people are less verbose); and use a timer (e.g. an egg timer, to keep all calls to a maximum of four minutes). Do not be afraid to put a block on incoming calls to reduce interruptions.
5. If you have an assistant, use him or her to deal with or to redirect (helpfully) any mail or callers (whether in person or on the telephone), where he/she or someone else could better deal with them. Strive for excellence and not perfection through your assistant.
6. Apply these principles to emailing, to avoid your day becoming too fragmented by responding to a steady drip of incoming messages.

How do you value other people's time?

It is vital to develop not only a personal sense of time, but also a sense of the value of other people's time.

How do I measure up as a manager or mismanager of other people's working capital of time?

For example you shouldn't frequently interrupt other people's meetings or assume that your telephone call to them is a welcome interruption. Missing deadlines, keeping people waiting, talking at great length at meetings – all these indicate that you don't view other people's time as precious.

Idea 99: Making time to think

It is essential for the leader to make time to think, both about the present and the future. That means in the first place an awareness of the value of time and the economical use of it.

> *What advice can be offered to a leader? He must discipline himself and lead a carefully regulated and ordered life. He must allow a certain amount of time for quiet thought and reflection; the best times are in the early morning, and in the evening. The quality, good or bad, of any action which is to be taken will vary directly with the time spent in thinking; against this, he must not be rigid; his decisions and plans must be readily adaptable to changing situations. A certain ruthlessness is essential, particularly with inefficiency and also with those who would waste his time. People will accept this, provided the leader is ruthless with himself...*
>
> *Most leaders will find there is so much to do and so little time to do it; that was my experience in the military sphere. My answer to that is not to worry; what is needed is a quiet contemplation of all aspects of the problem, followed by a decision – and it is fatal to worry afterwards.*
>
> Field Marshal Viscount Montgomery

Idea 100: How to manage meetings

Before holding any meeting, ask yourself these five questions:

1. Why are we meeting?
2. What would be the result of not having the meeting, or what should result from having it?
3. Who should attend?
4. How long should it be and how should it be structured?
5. When is the best time to hold it?

There are five types of meeting:

1. *Briefing* meetings – to impart and share information, to clarify points and incorporate ideas from others.
2. *Advisory* meetings – to gather views and advice and to outline or share any ideas.
3. *Council* meetings – to make and share responsibility for decisions, resolving differences on the way.
4. *Committee* meetings – to 'vote' on decisions and reach compromises/accommodations of different views on matters of common concern.
5. *Negotiating* meetings – to reach decisions by bargaining with other parties who are acting in their own best interest.

You should decide what each type of meeting you are to be involved with actually is and plan to run each type as time efficiently as possible, depending on their purpose.

Having decided that a meeting is really necessary, you should consider how much of your time (and other people's) the subject of it is worth. It should then begin and end on time. You should manage a

meeting to ensure that progress is made and action decided. It is vital to get the involvement of all present (or else why are they there?) and end on a positive note.

Being aware of the cost of meetings will focus the mind and planning will focus your actions. Minutes to record actions agreed and responsibilities should be in a form that gives ease of follow-up and subsequent checking.

These are the hallmarks of successfully managed meetings:

- Meetings are planned ahead for who should attend and with the agenda and any useful papers being circulated in advance.
- Times for each item and the meeting itself are set in advance (and adhered to).
- Minutes are concise and action oriented (with responsibilities allocated).
- There is clarity of outcomes (shared by all).
- Meetings are reviewed continually for effectiveness.
- The focus is on the positive.
- You are a successful umpire and referee.

Is this meeting really necessary? If it is, make sure that you lead it effectively.

Follow-up test

Effective communication

- ☐ Do you believe in the central importance of good two-way communication in the context of working life?
- ☐ Before any formal communication situation – such as a presentation or a meeting – do you consider the six principles of effective speaking?
- ☐ Can you speak clearly, simply and concisely, and also do so with spirit and in a natural unselfconscious way?
- ☐ Are your skills of preparing and planning consistently applied to interviews and meetings?
- ☐ Has anyone commented in the last six months that you are a good listener?
- ☐ Can you take constructive criticism in the right spirit and manner as well as give it?
- ☐ In your organization, are there clear if informal channels for downward, upward and lateral communication?
- ☐ Are they clogged up with weeds, or clear, fresh and in daily use?

Managing your time

- ☐ Do you know where your time goes?
- ☐ Can you handle interruptions effectively?
- ☐ Do you have problems in chairing meetings?
- ☐ Do you have a system for dealing with telephone calls, emails and paperwork?

- ☐ Do you always plan the day and prioritize the tasks to be done?
- ☐ Are there other ways in which you could organize your personal working life – for example how you deal with any personal administration – in order to be a more effective leader?
- ☐ Do you delegate sufficiently? Can you delegate more? Can you give more discretion over decisions and more accountability to a sub-group or individual?
- ☐ Can you identify at least three steps you can take now in order to become a better organizer of your time?

  i

  ii

  iii
- ☐ Do you need more time to think, time for your team, and time for your key customers, partners and allies?
- ☐ Can you give yourself a mark out of ten for each of the ten principles of time management?
- ☐ What practical steps have you identified to improve your score over the next six months?
- ☐ Would you agree that the biggest time-waster in your life is the person you see every day in the mirror?
- ☐ Does the urgent tend to drive out the important in your daily work? If so, what do you now plan to do about it?
- ☐ Do you accept that a significant amount of stress is often a symptom of poor time management skills?

It is not enough to be busy – what matters is what you are busy about.

About John Adair

John Adair is the business guru who invented Action Centred Leadership (ACL) in the 1970s, now one of the best known leadership models in the world. Organisations worldwide use it to develop their leadership capability and management skills. ACL is being successfully applied in engineering companies, retailers, local authorities, financial institutions and universities. The British armed services base their leadership training upon it.

John's company, Adair International, provides ACL development programmes, Accredited Trainer programmes and consultancy around the world, via regional partnerships with training providers in the UK, Australia, New Zealand, the Middle East and India.

John is the author of more than 40 books, translated into many languages, and numerous articles on history, leadership and management development.

Index

ALSO AVAILABLE...

9780857081155

9780857081148

9780857081308

9780857081315

9780857081018

9780857081506

9780857082046

...and there's more to come!